Ian Niall's
Complete Angler

IAN NIALL

Ian Niall's
Complete Angler

Illustrated with drawings by
MEIRION ROBERTS

and with
photographs

BOOK CLUB ASSOCIATES
LONDON

This edition published 1976 by
Book Club Associates
By arrangement with William Heinemann Ltd

Metrication: *In common with current angling journals, the weight of
fish is measured in pounds and ounces in this book*

Printed Offset Litho and bound in Great Britain
by Cox & Wyman Ltd
London, Fakenham and Reading

Contents

Glossary

Back-bone	a certain stiffness from butt to tip of the rod.
Birds' nests	tangles of nylon caused by the line kinking.
Brandling	an earthworm.
Bungs	the name given to large floats, often painted orange or bright red, used in pike fishing with live or dead bait.
Cloudbait	any kind of milled or crushed 'flour', such as biscuit crumb, used to attract fish to the swim without giving much to feed upon.
Coarse fish	a term applied to our native species of fish found in fresh water lakes, ponds, streams, etc, excluding members of the salmon family, sea trout, brown trout and salmon.
Disgorger	a double-pronged or notched rod or metal strip which is pushed into the mouth of the fish to prise the hook free without damaging or killing the fish.
Float	any means of floating the line on the surface and holding the bait in position in the water below. Floats are sometimes goose quills, wood and cork, or plastic.
Float-ledger	a combination of a float and ledger.
Fly	in the strictest sense of the word, an imitation of a natural insect taken by fish such as trout, sea trout, chub or perch. A salmon fly is a lure.
Free-lining	allowing the bait to be carried to the fish without impediment of lead or weight of any kind to cause drag.
Fry	any small fish that is less than about two inches in length and has yet to grow and mature.

Gaff	a large barbless hook, generally with a gape of two inches or more, fastened to a handle to enable a newly-caught fish to be lifted out of the water.
Gag	a very necessary device incorporating a loop of spring steel and fashioned like a pair of tongs which, when inserted into the mouth of a pike, keeps the jaws apart, while the hook is removed with the aid of a disgorger.
Game fish	salmon, sea trout and brown trout.
Keep net	a net of perhaps four or five feet in length with a wire frame. The open end of the net is pegged to the bank and kept clear of the water. The lower part of the net is submerged. Fish which are caught are then kept until they may be examined and weighed before being returned to the water.
Landing net	a poke-shaped net with a handle used to lift out newly-caught fish of a size that can be handled in this way.
Ledger	the baited line being weighted to keep the bait on the bottom by passing the line through a lead. When the fish takes the bait he feels no resistance until the weight lifts, a 'stop' in the form of a swivel coming up against it and preventing any further line being drawn through the weight.
Lie	a place where a fish takes up a feeding place or 'lies' waiting for food or the right amount of water to come down to allow it to ascend to the spawning ground.
Lure	anything made of wood, metal, feathers, bone, etc. to imitate the food of predatory fish.
Margin-fishing	setting out to fish the pond or lake close to the bank and not laying out a long line beyond the shallow water.
Netted	the use of the landing net to remove fish from the water.
Ottering	the illegal use of a weighted board drifted to carry a string of flies over trout in a river or lake.
Paternoster	a device generally made of brass wire but sometimes of heavy nylon incorporating two, three or more booms from which baited hooks are strung. A weight at the end keeps the baited hooks off the bottom when a tight line is fished to enable this to be done, keeping the bait out of the reach of crabs and other bottom feeders.
Plankton	micro organisms. A minute form of organic life, which grows and develops in water, attracting crustaceans and small fish, sand-eels etc., upon which larger fish feed.
Plug	a plug-shaped lure made of wood or plastic having a lip which causes it to dive deeper in the water when retrieved quickly.

Priest	the name given to a club of metal or heavy wood used to kill a fish quickly and avoid its suffocating in air when it has been removed from the water.
Rafting	the use of a small wooden raft fitted with a sail in order to carry a line with a number of baited hooks over a likely feeding place off the shore or beach (illegal used on fresh water).
Run	flowing water between one pool or fish's resting place and another.
Sallow	a species of low-growing willow.
Seine net	a fine mesh net suitably weighted so that it can be submerged in the water, taken out by a boatman or handled by an operator on the opposite bank, to capture shoals of fish to be taken out and removed or tagged and measured and returned.
Shot	lead of varying sizes, cast like a pellet but with a slit which enables it to be pressed onto the line and clamped there to act as a tiny weight and sink the line to the required fishing depth.
Sink-and-draw	the practice of casting a fly or bait, allowing it to sink to the bottom and rest there to attract a fish and then drawing the bait or fly on to lure whatever fish may lie in its path.
Slater	name for a wood louse.
Spinners	revolving lures.
Spoons	spoon-shaped lures which turn and undulate in the water.
Swim	the territory of particular species of fish while they are patrolling in search of food or shoaling.
Tailer	a device with a handle similar to the handle of the landing net but having a running noose of wire which is slid over the tail of a large salmon or sea-trout in order to remove it from the water after it has been caught on rod and line.
Trace	a length of nylon or fine wire used between the line and the spoon, lure, fly or bait – wire in the case of pike and other fish capable of 'sawing' through nylon.
Trolling	towing a lure of any kind behind a boat, the lure being weighted to keep it down in the water.
Wading staff	a stick with a thong to go over the wrist – enables the angler to walk comfortably over rocky river bed without too much danger of slipping and falling in.

1

The Angler's Point of View

It may be that you already know something about fish and fishing and are attracted by something more than just catching a fish. There is a lot of excitement in using special tackle and luring fish with particular methods, but we must begin at the beginning.

Angling is a subject that can be defined quite simply as fishing with a rod, and everyone who fishes with a rod is an angler of sorts. But angling is more than sitting on a bank with a rod and line waiting for a fish to take the bait. Where to fish, how to fish, what tackle to use and, equally important, when to fish, are the really important parts of the education of the angler.

There is always more to learn about angling. Those who have fished all their lives will tell you that. At the same time it is possible to overlook what can seem obvious. Fish don't live by rule books, nor can they be caught to order. If there was no element of luck in fishing it would be a very dull, unexciting sport.

Between beginner's luck and the high degree of skill of the expert there is much to be studied. If a fish doesn't recognize the tackle and bait dropped into the water by the expert it can certainly be frightened away by the unsuitable bait or the clumsily rigged-up tackle of the novice.

Long ago man hunted with a spear. His quarry wasn't only the wild boar or the fleet-hoofed antelope but the fish of the lake and river. Nets and harpoons were used but there were places where fish were not easily harpooned and the net could not be used. The fish hook, lashed to a length of line, was the answer, but the line often tangled in reeds and bushes and there were ponds and pools where it had to be carried over obstructions by the use of a stick or pole. The fisherman thus discovered angling and went on improving tackle and technique. He had to, because the fish were learning their lessons from experience, too.

When a float dips or a rod point trembles as a fish takes the bait it doesn't always mean that a fish can be lifted on to the bank. Every angler talks about the fish that gets away. Most of these fish later grow bigger in the mind. The angler doesn't think about the lesson he is giving the fish, even though his behaviour gradually teaches the fish something about the business.

Tame fish begin to associate certain things with danger. Older fish will take longer to swallow the bait. Fish that escape are frightened and disturbances leave their mark upon them, just as an otter plunging into a shoal is recalled with fear every time the animal leaves a wake when it swims across a pool.

Before you arm yourself with a rod you must consider what sort of fishing you want to do. Coarse fish? Game fish? Or sea fish? We shall consider them all in detail.

There are so many different kinds of rods that books could be written about them alone, without mentioning reels, lines, or what is used at the end of the line! The rod was once no more than a means to an end. Now it is a specialized implement, designed for fishing in the sea, the river or the lake. Length of rod, diameter, action and materials all vary.

The rod for bait-fishing for a pike might well serve to throw out a paternoster used for sea fishing, but it would be quite useless for fly-fishing or for catching roach, rudd, chub or mullet. A long match rod would never do for sea fishing. A delicate fly rod would be ruined by a pike and the pike would never be brought to the bank.

The match rod is long because the match angler has to fish out beyond bushes and must set up his rod at a peg on the bank. His is the luck of the draw. The long rod is soft-tipped. The match angler must detect a bite immediately. He is generally fishing for small fish. His prize depends on making weight, and small fish may barely make the soft tip of that long rod move. They are there and then suddenly away in the batting of an eye, but a really big fish might be hard to bring in and time would be lost. Waiting for him to take the bait could cost the fisherman a score of small fish with perhaps greater weight altogether than the cautious giant who nosed around for so long.

The sea rod that is to be used from a boat must be strong enough to haul up a skate that hugs the bottom and seems as heavy as a grand piano. But it must not be too long or its use from the boat will be cancelled out when the fish is able to keep his distance, so avoiding the gaff or the landing net. This short rod, on the other hand, will be a handicap when used from a beach. It won't lever a bait out high enough and far enough to get well beyond the surf as the big, two-handed beach-casting rod does.

Beach rods, boat rods, pier fishing rods, rock fishing rods, more delicate spinning rods for mackerel and bass, fine rods for mullet, and powerful rods to work a conger out from a cavern where he has his tail well wrapped around a column of stone or a suitable boulder – the choice bewilders the novice. Even the average sea fisherman will be at a loss to know how many rods he needs and only the specialist will be happy, thinking of only one species of fish.

Almost as difficult to decide upon is the reel to be used. Here again there are many designs, some with distinct advantages over others and most with their own drawbacks. There are fly reels that run on ball-bearings and others that are comparatively simple affairs.

The latest refinement is a reel which, at the pressure of a finger, retrieves the line and to some extent plays the fish. The simple revolving drum (inspired by the wheel) has many uses. It may be widened to take more line, contracted and increased in diameter to reel in two or three hundred yards of stout sea line. It may be able to run free to make casting easier, and have a variable ratchet to control the line recovery.

FIXED-SPOOL REEL

This is only the beginning of the range of choice in reels and reel designs. There is the fixed-spool reel, a device that has revolutionized angling. The fixed-spool reel is what its name implies. The reel doesn't turn. Line spills over the lip of the spool when a bale-arm is pressed back out of the way. The weight of the tackle or the spinner at the end of the line straightens the line itself.

The only drawback is that the line tends to become twisted as it goes out. In theory this twist is reversed as the line is re-spooled by a shuttling action and the turning of the bale-arm mechanism, the only part of the reel that revolves except the winding handle and gears.

In practice things rarely work out quite so smoothly. Without some care in the choice of line and the tackle used, a greater kink may be imparted to the coils being spooled. No one uses a spinning reel for long without making birds' nests if the spinner and weights happen to be too heavy, the swivels stick, or the tackle is too much for the diameter of line being used.

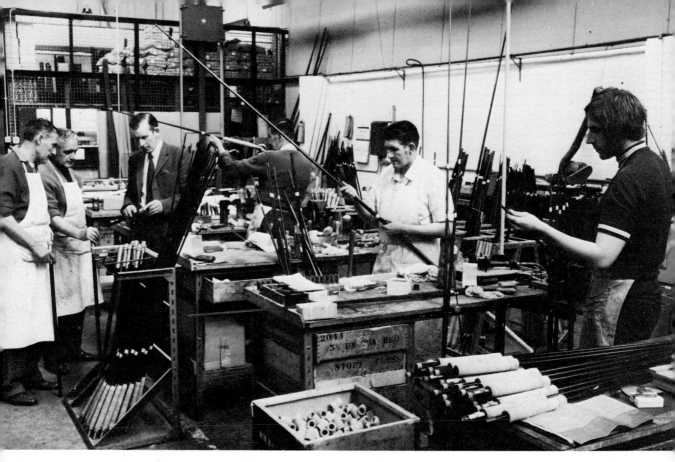

Hardy's of Alnwick, Northumberland, produce a wide range of top quality
fibreglass

(Hardy's)

The multiplier is certainly a highly efficient design of reel. It is a sophisticated development of the everyday revolving drum reel. Its refinement lies in a mechanism which enables the line to be recovered much faster than the ordinary reel, generally a four to one ratio. The gearing makes the drum turn four times to one turn of the handle. A rapid recovery is matched by a very smooth release of line.

The drum can be freed to turn as the line and the weight at the end go sailing out. Tackle can be dropped into the water with great precision but the beginner needs to practise. Even with a drag or brake which can be applied to the free-running drum it is possible, again mainly by lack of judgement in the matter of weight and distance, to get what are known as over-runs, line merrily pouring off the drum after the tackle is in the water.

The result of over-run is that a spinner falls to the bottom and may be firmly fixed in rock or weed by the time the line is sorted out and rewound. A hooked fish may take off and wind line round obstacles to tear himself free. Even old hands become almost demented when this kind of thing happens.

The solution lies in practice and careful study of the balancing of tackle, particularly in different conditions of water and weather when high winds or heavy currents make casting and retrieving more difficult.

If you have chosen to fly fish for trout you will equip yourself with a fly rod of split cane or fibreglass and a simple fly reel. Additional equipment will be a landing net, a fly box stocked with flies and perhaps some line grease to float the line. If you are pike fishing then items you will need in addition to your much more robust rod (which again may be of fibreglass), your fixed spool or multiplier reel, will be spinners, dead bait and a gaff with which to lift the fish from the water. The pike should always be gaffed in the gills so that he can be put back without having been damaged. You will also need a pike gag to keep his jaws open while you recover your hook. Even the gills of a pike are armed with fine needle-like teeth!

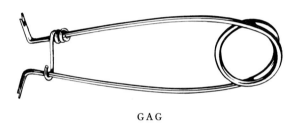

GAG

If you are fishing for such coarse fish as chub, bream, roach, rudd, carp or tench then you may choose lighter rods and finer lines, which we shall talk about in due course, but you will also take with you a landing net and perhaps a stool, a fishing basket and even an umbrella to shelter you from the rain. Roach fishing and sometimes bream fishing require long vigils by the water. Carp fishing may keep you out all night!

You will also have a keep net – one of the essential pieces of equipment for the coarse fisherman. Every self-respecting coarse fisherman puts the fish he catches into a keep net. It is a stout affair made of wire rings upon which the net is fixed to form a sort of tunnel that stretches from the angler's perch on the bank down into the water of the river or pond. The captured fish can swim about in the net and come to no harm. At the end of the day they are freed and the stock is never depleted.

Having gathered the basic equipment for the sort of angling you have chosen to do, you must consider the fish and where it is to be found. The pike is one of the predators of the world of fishes, a hawk or a falcon who rushes after his prey, gorges it and settles back in the reeds while his heavy meal digests. Sometimes he chases comparatively large fish. Sometimes he will dine on small fry.

Pike will rarely be found in complete isolation from any other species; but the perch, which, like many other kinds of fish, is predatory, can live in a pond where there are only perch. Perch will eat perch, of course, just as big trout will eat small trout.

Apart from the predatory fish there are many that do no more than sift the mud for worms, larvae and beetles, as the bream does. The roach too is a more delicate feeder and neither likes fast water. Indeed, sluggish water is much more to the liking of the bream and the roach. Carp, too, are still-water fish and tench stay where they are, mainly in ponds and silty lakes with no great inflow or outflow. The trout, on the other hand, is a fish that lies in muddy, sluggish water and thrives only in clear streams where the weed is continually washed by the flow of fresh water.

Even fishing in the sea, along the estuary of the river or around the pier, you will have to think of the ways and habits of the fish you are hoping to catch. Flounders, dabs, plaice and skate, too, keep away from rocky or shingle-strewn beaches, for the simple reason that their particular food is only to be had on sandy areas or the silt of estuaries into which lugworms burrow and razor fish retreat. On the edges of weed beds you will find those fish that live on prawns and small fry. In the rocky caverns there will be sinuous congers lurking to seize other fish that feed on tiny crabs and other crustaceans. Fish where the fish are, and fish with imagination.

As important as anything in fishing is your approach to the water. Here so many beginners go wrong. Fishing with a rod and line may not look the same sort of thing as stalking a deer, but it is. The angler who takes care not to disturb the water, not to let himself be seen, catches most fish. Think of the heron and see how this bird takes fish. It would have become extinct if it hadn't learned

how to keep still. It walks slowly. It moves gracefully into the water. It stands still for minutes on end. It waits for the fish to pass by. The fish may have caught a glimpse of the heron as it stepped down the bank, but the passing of time makes them less wary. They are hungry and they soon feed again in the shallows. The heron spears one and walks up out of the water to swallow it on the bank. It moves on. Instinct tells it to fish a little farther along. The frightened shoal has gone upstream perhaps. The heron, you will notice, is not exactly white, nor black in sharp contrast to the background of the sky, but blue-grey. It stands like some clump of weed on the side of the bank. It blends with the bushes, the reeds, the hill behind it. It is, in fact, almost invisible to the fish. Think of this and remember how many fishermen you see wearing the wrong sort of clothes, white shirts, bright anoraks, things that make them conspicuous to other people, let alone a fish that looks up at the sky, continually alert for items of food or the approach of danger!

You may sing as loudly as you wish. Fish are largely insulated from the sound of your voice by the blanket of water above them, but water is a good conductor. Vibration resulting from your boot striking a rock, an oar being dropped into the boat or some similar shocking sound, is quickly conveyed to the fish and away it goes, out of the danger zone, frightening or warning other fish as it goes. You will never know what fish were there before you alarmed them. Shoals move as one. Big fish have their hiding places. Once alarmed, it is a long time before they venture back into open water.

It requires only a little common sense to understand how much an angler benefits from being careful in his approach. Remember that a shoal may have hundreds of eyes and a shadow on the water is all that is needed to disperse the shoal in all directions. A footfall on the bank will send fish into cover long before you have set up your rod. Fish will see you or detect your presence by the disturbance you make. You must be as hard to spot as the heron, and equally as still. Some anglers say that a good fisherman needs to think like a fish, but fish do not think. They react to danger. A trout that gets off the hook will sometimes put his head in a hole under a rock and leave his body in full view. If the angler thought like a fish he wouldn't be thinking at all! What he must do is to use imagination and think of the reaction of fish, having studied them before putting up a rod.

2
The World of the Fish

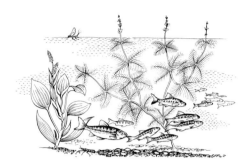

The flies that dance above the water are the reason why there are fish down below. The jellyfish that slowly drifts past as you sit on a rock admiring the water means the presence of mackerel shoals.

The world of the fish is hidden from us. It is hard to see into any but the clearest of waters, and clear water, unless it is quite deep, is shunned by most species of fish.

The underwater world of the migrating salmon consists of a number of mooring places, or salmon lies, to which the fish ascending the river moves when the flood is enough to let him pass through what are normally shallows. The salmon doesn't feed in fresh water. He reacts instinctively to the sorts of things he ate while in the sea, and can be lured. He is, however, caught with worms, although rarely by a single worm, and usually on a bunch of worms fastened on a hook to resemble something like a squid or a miniature octopus. Apart from the salmon, other game fish, and all coarse fish, must feed in order to live and maintain their condition.

The difference between what are known as coarse fish and game fish is that the former spawn in summer. Game fish, salmon, sea trout and brown trout begin to spawn in late autumn and continue to do so in winter. It is for this reason, and in the interests of conserving the species, that laws governing the taking of fish in the spawning season apply to fishing and fishermen.

Coarse fish is a reasonable name for most of the fish that spawn in summer, for few of them are really edible or welcomed by the cook. It is true that a baked pike that is not too large (a jack) can be quite good to eat, and a freshly caught perch is sometimes as tasty as any trout, but in the main the coarse fish is bony and often inclined to have the flavour of mud.

The world of the trout, sea trout and salmon, and that in-between grayling, which is a very handsome and edible coarse fish, is one of pure water. None of these can survive very long in water that has a high sediment content. They suffocate or become sick in polluted rivers. They shun the slow-flowing, sluggish stream because there, in spite of insects and larvae upon which trout and grayling could live, they would die from lack of oxygen.

The trout cannot adjust to heavy mud or the presence of insoluble materials continually stirred up by the inflow of drains, feeder streams and ditches. It lives where its particular kind of food is plentiful, feeding on flies, beetles, grubs, small fry and even the ova of its own kind.

You will discover that trout rise at certain times and only very occasionally feed throughout the day. There is what is called the rise, a time, perhaps once in the morning and again in the late afternoon or evening, when the rings of rising fish can be seen on the stream or the water of the lake.

This is not because all trout are hungry at the same moment. It means that larvae are passing through a stage of development, breaking the skin which encased them as nymphs and appearing on the surface as newly-hatched flies.

All this began perhaps a year ago. The flies you saw dancing above the water sometimes dropped to the surface to lay eggs. The eggs tumbled down to the river bed and remained there, developing into larvae. Finally these became the nymphs, which, on a warm evening or summer's morning, rose to the surface to emerge as flies, ready to mate and in turn to lay eggs on the water.

Between the development of the larvae and the rising of the nymph to break the surface, the trout feed, first on the river bed, then in mid-water and then on the surface. The rings are an indication that the trout is taking either the nymph or the hatching fly. But the trout also feeds on the bottom, pursuing beetles.

When insects are scarce, towards the end of the year, there are alevins (the newly-developed ova of spawning trout) to feed upon, and finally the fry and the fingerlings into which these alevins grow. The world of the trout is a jungle in which the strong prey upon the weak.

In a similar way fish that live in less turbulent water and places where there is hardly any current, live on insect life, water snails, grubs, larvae, beetles, the ova and fry of their own, or some other species.

Like the brown trout, which is not brown but varies in colour from olive green to a rich yellow and is sometimes silver and dotted with the most beautiful red marks, the coarse fish matches the background of the world in which it lives.

The sun glints on the dark grey muds of a slow-flowing canal or lake and here, in the deeps, swim bream. The bream searches the muds for the pea mussel, the water slater, which is something like the dry-land wood louse, worms and larvae as well as snails. The common bream is a wonderful golden brown or bronze. He is deep-bodied. His mouth is specially designed for sifting the mud to extract the larvae of midges called bloodworms.

The bream will feed standing on his head and waving his tail as he takes in mud and blows it out again. He might be called a riverbed scavenger. In winter he prefers the deeps and, as always, he seeks the company of his own kind.

The jungle has its tiger in the long grass. The pike feeds on whatever comes his way. He has a great burst of speed but like the short-winged hawk in the air, he doesn't pursue his quarry or even attempt to catch a fish that has a good start.

The bittern, a bird that sometimes haunts the fen in which the pike swims, is known as a down-looker. Its eyes are so placed in its skull that when it seems to be looking over the marsh it is actually watching the water immediately below its beak.

The pike then, is an 'up-looker'. His eyes are so placed in his skull that he looks towards the surface of the water. He sees what passes above, rather than beneath him. He waits for the shoal. The pike is camouflaged like a leopard. His green skin is flecked with white or pale yellow. He blends with the pattern of the place beneath him. He looks like the green weeds and the dapples of sunlight seen on the bottom.

The pike has a body like a torpedo. His pectoral fins are broad and capable of thrusting him forward like a rocket. His anal fin is a keel. His broad tail keeps him perfectly balanced. His mouth opens so wide that he can take a fish of almost his own size. His teeth all slant towards his gullet so that anything he holds can rarely be released and must be torn from his mouth.

The pike's purpose in the world of fish is to eliminate the slow and the sickly. Those that survive his dash into the shoal or manage to elude him by taking cover in close-growing weeds are always strong, healthy specimens. Greedy though he may seem, he has long spells of apathy when he cannot be tempted.

Lesser fish seem to know when the pike is on the move, just as small birds can tell the intention of a hawk. But the pike will sometimes spend days brooding. What is actually happening is that his body is absorbing food. His stomach acid, which is very powerful stuff, is breaking down some large item which he bolted days before.

In months when the water temperature is high, the pike seems to sleep with his eyes open. He even acquires a fine coating of silt on some occasions. He is then so unaware of the world that the river keeper has no difficulty in slipping a snare wire over his tail and hoisting him out onto the bank with the aid of a long pole.

Pike will pursue pike. They will follow the duck swimming across the pond accompanied by her brood of ducklings, picking off the dappled youngsters one by one like a submarine stalking a convoy of merchant ships.

Take the pike away, as some river keepers do, and the quality of the fish and fishing gets worse. One gamekeeper snared and speared pike to give his hatching mallard a better chance.

There are few things the pike won't go for. He has been known to seize a shot pheasant that dropped in the river. There are legends of him taking a pony by the muzzle, seizing the hand of a maid washing clothes in a pool. He has been caught with some strange baits, including a dead Labrador puppy fastened to a specially forged hook on a line made of heavy picture wire.

The truth about the pike is that he is a fresh-water shark with the shark's small brain. He is as hard to kill as a shark or a conger eel. I remember catching a small one of about five pounds which I had thought quite dead but which revived when being prepared for the oven, after travelling more than sixty miles in the boot of a car, and being out of the water for six hours.

The pike lives in the river, the lake, the pond and the canal so that he may hunt roach and rudd, dace, minnows and other small fry. He is not averse to frogs and voles. The mouse that tumbles into the pool will do, or the moorhen's chick. He will go for anything that moves. He doesn't care whether it is a piece of cloth on a hook or a long-dead herring. He is master of his particular beat or stretch of water and will not tolerate lesser pike in his swim.

To be a successful pike fisherman you must know the pike just as you must know the trout, the carp or the bream if you would catch them.

The carp is one of the most exciting of the fresh-water fishes, not just because he is known to grow to a very large size, equal to that of some of the best pike ever taken, but because of his shyness and his nocturnal habit.

The excited carp angler talks of carp wallowing in the clearing in the weeds and looking as big as a pig. The sudden appearance of a carp close to the surface or breaking the moonlit water is enough to stop a man's heart beating. A glimmer of light on the fish is enough to grip the angler's imagination and make the fish look twice its size.

The sound of the carp's surfacing, a waving of his tail if he upends to bore at something in the mud, is quite paralysing. The novice carp fisherman has to study how to keep his nerve. By the time he has got over the shock the carp is away! There was probably nothing he could have done about it in any case, for catching a carp is like laying an ambush or even planning a battle. When the carp has moved the die is cast. He has either taken the bait laid out for him, or gone on looking for something more natural.

The carp was a fish the Romans liked. It was almost certainly brought to parts of Europe where the legions established themselves. It became a stock fish in the monastery stew – the lake or pond attached to the religious settlement to provide fish for Friday, the day upon which the good monks did without meat.

Stew-ponds were also set up by the owners of country estates. Many of these ponds still exist even in places where the mansion has crumbled and fallen in ruin.

The carp is capable of living to a considerable age. He thrives best where worms that live in mud or silt are most plentiful.

Like the bream, another stew-pond fish, he enjoys the snail and the fly larvae, but, fortunately for the carp fisherman, he will take a number of baits not at all like the items on his everyday menu, such as potatoes and bread crust. He moves out of the dense weed, the impenetrable jungle of submerged roots and water-logged trees, at nightfall. A few lesser carp are to be found in what are sometimes called cow-ponds, where the heavily weeded water is rich in insect life of all kinds.

The perch, on the other hand, is sometimes called the small boy's fish. He is easily caught from the shoal, although larger perch live a solitary life and are not so easily caught.

When the shoaling perch are hungry they rush at a dangled worm like fierce terriers and will have a tug-of-war over the worm that is torn from the hook. It is possible to catch them at every cast when they are in the mood, but all at once, as with the rising trout, the shoaling perch stop feeding. The shoal swims gently on, dallying here and there, nosing in the weed forest, swimming up-stream and making leisurely progress towards some new resting place out of the main flow of the current.

The big perch is rather like the pike. He feeds when he is hungry and waits for something worth having to come into view, such as a preoccupied crayfish, a small roach or a wriggling company of elvers on migration.

Watch the perch and you will discover how he bristles at the approach of other fish, his sharp dorsal fin stiffening to discourage a pike from seizing him. (Even a pike may let the perch go when the spines of that dorsal fin stick fast in the roof of his mouth.)

The perch is an aggressive fish and a very handsome fellow. Young ones hide against the stalks of weeds, their five-barred flanks making them almost invisible in the pattern of stems and shadows. As the perch becomes older these barred markings disappear, however. The fish becomes a loner and takes his own station on the edge of the weeds where he can be fished for by the angler who knows where to find him.

If the perch never attains the size of the pike, the carp or even the bream, pound for pound he matches them for dash and fight, and none looks better in the net.

Although you will rarely do as well at low water as you will when the river is normal or the tide is coming back, the most rewarding visit you may make to the shore, the lake, the gravel pit or pond, is at neap tide or in drought. When the water level has fallen you will see what the world of the fish looks like and be able to make a mental map of the area normally submerged.

Without some picture of what lies below, the angler is fishing blind. In drought, obstructions, water channels, boulders and other features of the river or lake bed are revealed. At low tide you may discover why bass always move along a certain course or mullet travel in a certain way going up with the tide. More than this, you will see why fish rise or may be hooked in certain places and not in others.

The flow of water controls the dispersal of food. Little remains where the current is strong, either food or fish. In the broad river you will discover that a trout rises in the same place no matter what the volume of water sweeping over the weir. The answer is that there is a depression on the riverbed, or an eddy behind a large boulder where the fish has his station. It takes effort and strength for a fish to fight the current and small items of food would be swept away before the fish could feed in the main stream. Food swirls into eddies and calmer areas behind rocks and in these places the fish can keep his station with little effort.

It is into these eddies and depressions that your bait or lure must be cast. You can only discover them by studying the riverbed in times of drought.

The underwater world has hollows, ridges, steps and even bushes and dead trees in the flooded pit or the reservoir that was once open countryside. Knowledge of this underwater 'landscape' is vital to the angler who would drop his bait into the company of feeding bream or intercept the chub sliding out from the shelter of the bushes in the dusk.

Just as there are haunts of rabbits, fox, badger and every other sort of land animal, there are haunts of different kinds of fish. These haunts take much longer to discover by trial and error than just by careful survey when the water level permits. Small fish are found in shallows and behind small rocks in streamy runs. Good fish need cover and more water over their backs. Fishing blind may be fishing with imagination, but the imagination blossoms when you know what is there, unseen, beneath the still water of the pond, the canal or the lake.

Once you know where the fish live you may have a key to why they station themselves there. It is often also the key to their feeding habits.

3
The Lures

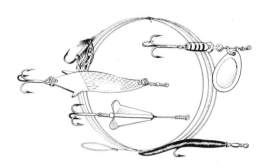

It is possible to catch fish with a lure because of their natural reaction and predatory habit. Most fish, except the more sluggish and sedentary bottom feeders, will move in pursuit of something that resembles natural prey.

The lure must have a lifelike action and, as far as possible, be made to move naturally. You can buy many sorts of lure. Some, their makers claim, set up a vibration which stimulates the hungry fish to rush at them. Others look so like fish that it is almost impossible to distinguish between the imitation and the living fish.

There are earthworms as soft as the freshly-dug, broadtailed earthworm, but equipped, of course, with hooks. There are pliable shrimps, prawns, neat little fish that wriggle along and dart and dive as the line is retrieved. There are spoons that wobble and spoons that sway as well as spinners that go fussily through the deeps looking like tiny fry trying to catch up with the shoal, but left far behind.

There are imitation sand-eels with propellers and minnows made of wood as well as every kind of plastic and metal alloy.

Some of these lures have been specially designed for trout, others for salmon, for pike or bass. There are also spoons that carry bait for the flounder. No cook ever had such a variety of spoons in her kitchen.

The design of a good lure is based upon the living creature best suited to catch particular fish.

There is one very important consideration in fishing the lure. It must, whether by intention or accident, pass before the fish in a way so natural that the fish isn't put off by the oddity of a shining piece of metal. The vital thing is the movement of the lure.

A good pike ready for the gaff

(Ken Whitehead)

The size of the lure is all important. It isn't hard to understand that a small fish may be put off by the approach of a lure as big as itself. Large fish will take the smallest of lures but they cannot be relied upon to do so on every occasion.

Where do we begin on the matter of lures? To include the sorts of fishing 'fly' that fall into this category would be to list a great many of the trout fisherman's favourites, and all the flies used for salmon.

What is a fishing fly? A fly is primarily the produce of the fly-tyer's art. It may be the imitation of a living insect, or a lure which the fish mistakes for a small fish, a minnow for instance, or trout fry. It may, on the other hand, be something that looks like a fresh-water shrimp. Many salmon flies are undoubtedly based upon the *salt-water* shrimp or prawn. Since fish live in a world of monochrome the colours employed in the lure have no other purpose than to match the particular shade a salmon sees when it looks at a living prawn.

The fly-tyer, however, fashions his flies like a witch mixing a brew. There are charms and superstitions about flies. The 'recipes' call for some very exotic ingredients from the fibres of the macaw's tail and the golden pheasant's crest to the feather of the jungle cock. These altogether add up to something that would make fine dress ornaments or costume jewellery.

What the fish sees has been overlooked, but the fly is successful so long as the tone range is reasonably good and the lure is not too big (or too little) when the water calls for one thing or the other.

The subject of flies or lures for salmon fills books, but the experienced salmon angler knows that two or three are all he needs, and size matters above all else.

The trout fly that is properly a lure always has a touch of silver or gold about it to attract the attention of a fish from a distance and often a little flare of red or crimson to simulate the gills of the tiny fish it is meant to represent. Such flies as the Peter Ross or the Butcher are well-known trout lures. They are fished beneath the surface of the water rather than on the top. Most salmon lures have even more colourful names – Black Dose, Green Highlander, Hairy Mary, Yellow Dog, Thunder and Lightning, Blue Charm, Marr Lodge, and many others.

It is necessary to divide lures into categories, for there are some that are simply allowed to sail through the water like the salmon fly, and others that are drawn along, causing them to duck and rise, sway or spin. The metal lures that simply react to the pressure of the water by swaying or diving are generally spoons. Spinners spin and Devon minnows revolve, usually at a high speed, which gives them a very fish-like appearance.

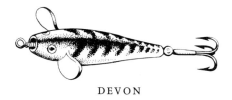

DEVON

The larger spoons may be several inches long. Devon minnows, which used to be highly thought of, have largely gone out of fashion nowadays. They were more expensive to produce and they gave place to a vibrating spinner with a torpedo-shaped body that looked every bit as good as the old-fashioned Devon minnows and caught fish equally as well.

The larger spoon was a thing our great-grandfathers used, mainly for pike. It was scaled down a bit and used for salmon, but it didn't come into its own until someone thought of giving it a fish shape and small fins, which improved its action. It was finally plated and all at once it was discovered to be the right thing for fish like salmon and pike, bass and mackerel.

Variations included making the spoon of copper, colouring it copper and gold, copper and black, silver and blue and so on. These spoons are to be had

SPOON

in a variety of sizes and weights. A heavy spoon is easier to cast, but of course it 'swims' deeper in the water.

The most popular dividing and swaying type of spoon at the moment is the Swedish Abu which has captured the market because the Swedes have done the most careful study of this type of lure. The silver Abu looks so like a wounded fish struggling through the water that it attracts more than the shoal over which it is fished. Even gulls will dive on it!

It incorporates a swivel, but as with all spinning tackle, one swivel alone is not advisable. A length of nylon and a second swivel should always link spinning tackle to the line proper. At the upper swivel it may be necessary to use a weight, sometimes to keep the spinner or spoon fishing evenly at the right depth and sometimes to prevent kink being imparted to the line.

The largest and heaviest Abu spoon may be used in the sea and will serve for pike. Occasionally one of the bigger spoons will take a salmon but in my experience the intermediate sizes are better. Salmon can be put off by the weight and size of the spoon. It must be remembered that a large spoon makes a greater vibration. In water of considerable depth a large spoon will do well. In shallow pools it makes a disturbance that outweighs its usefulness. There is a greater danger of snags and hang-ups when the heavy spoon is passing over rocks and other obstructions on the riverbed. Many an angler has tightened his line and been dismayed to find that what he was sure was a salmon was simply the heavy lure anchoring in a sunken branch or a slate ledge.

The popular revolving spoon that came into fashion in the late 1940s was of French origin. Frenchmen are great fishermen, makers of good reels and great inventors of lures like the Mepps and those little rubber 'fish' that have a life-like action.

The Mepps type spoon has a range of sizes to suit both fish and fishermen. The smallest may present some difficulty in casting without a lead on the trace. The larger sizes will take salmon and pike, although again the intermediate size is probably the most useful and it will do for bass and mackerel. Trout in the mill pool or lake will turn to it when the mood takes them.

Fishing with heavy lures one must be mindful that the weakest part of any tackle is at the knot. The knot to swivel that is most reliable is the half-blood knot. Remember at the same time that swivels should be of the right size, correspond with the swivel on the spoon if it comes equipped with swivel, and be free-running.

The purpose of swivels is to allow the spinner or spoon to turn without the line being twisted. This is barely possible when only one swivel is used. It is quite impossible when the spinner is heavy and drag on the line causes a swivel to bind. So two swivels are employed, one roughly eighteen inches ahead of the other.

Sometimes an angler may use a special forward swivel incorporating ball-bearings but this can be dispensed with by using anti-kink leads. Whatever items are incorporated in the rigging of tackle they always increase the danger of entanglement as the lure is drawn over weed or the fish runs with the hook firmly set in his jaw. The simplest linkage is the best – two good swivels on the trace with a spoon of the right weight.

Having set up your spinner, chosen the line to fish with, spooled it on the reel attached to the right kind of rod, there remains only the problem of how to spin.

In spinning the speed of recovery is of prime importance. Fish may give you only one chance and go down. They are put off when they have too long to study the slow-moving piece of chrome-plated metal, but it is also possible to fish too fast for pike and salmon. Pike, for instance, have a fast take-off but, like the hunting hawk, they give up quickly.

The spinner must travel at about the speed of a small fish of the same size. It must not be allowed to lag suddenly and sink in the water, for this doesn't happen when a pike gives chase. If the spinner drops in the water the fish in pursuit will slow down and perhaps sink with it to see why it behaves in this strange manner. It doesn't take long for the fish to discover what is different about this small, sick minnow. It is seen to have strange scales. Its eyes are daubs of paint. It has no taste – a fish's sense of taste is as acute as a dog's sense of smell.

How to spin realistically? Consider the water in which you are to spin. Is it fast-flowing or quite still? In fast-flowing water you need not retrieve with speed. The current will work the lure. The fish coming to it will have to fight the current. In water where the wind makes waves remember that down below the fish encounters very little pressure. In perfectly calm water the spinner must be retrieved with just enough pace to give it lifelike movement. A revolving spoon depends on its colours to create a general impression. A diving and swaying one will be fish-like in shape and almost always have some scale-like markings.

The plug bait is neither a spoon nor a spinner. It dives and rises because a front 'scoop' causes it to go down when it is towed with force and to rise when the pull slackens. Plugs can be given a very lifelike action. They do well in rivers where small fish may be hunted by pike, or a salmon may be irritated by something resembling the fish he fed upon in the sea.

Spinning enthusiasts either swear by plugs or have little time for them. Some of the simple plugs are most effective. They are generally equipped with a single treble hook, made of wood and painted green with a dab of red. Small simulated eyes may complete their decoration. The larger plugs have jointed bodies like the one illustrated. Some of the most lifelike plugs are those moulded

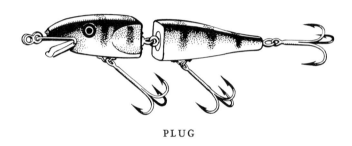

PLUG

in plastic or rubber. But, on the whole, plugs are not the main armament of the average spinning addict.

What of all the other sorts of lures to be seen in the tackle shops? There is no end to the choice. A great many of the devices offered were designed to catch the angler with money in his pocket rather than pike or bass.

There is another consideration which applies to spoons and spinning devices in general. Most of them can be made out of materials available to the do-it-yourself angler. Fishing spoons of different sorts can be fashioned from such things as old kitchen spoons and fork handles. It will be found that almost any plated object suitably bent or twisted will look fish-like in the water. It may have to be beaten into shape and altered a little, but it will lure the fish, particularly in the sea where shoals may tend to be more voracious than fish of the river or lake. Pike will even go for a piece of twisted tin. The angler will do well to remember that no fish can read the maker's name on the lure!

Talking about fish and the lure, we come to the mackerel and pollack fly, which, of course, isn't a fly at all but often no more than a dyed cock's feather whipped onto a hook.

Fishing from the beach the mackerel fisherman may set up a trace with half a dozen flies and a heavy weight. The rod is then lowered and lifted, lowered and lifted again so that the 'flies' appear to be whitebait or elvers rushing to the surface. Sometimes three or more mackerel may be caught at once.

Pollack too, take the fly in the same way. Bass, being a more wary species of fish, need to be approached with more care and offered a single fly of the kind used for sea trout or salmon. Again the fly is presented as a small fish or a prawn and in this case will only be an effective lure when bass are close to the surface.

The best indication for successful fly-fishing in the sea is the presence of whitebait or sand-eels shoaling in comparatively shallow water. This fact is often discovered by the flocking of gulls immediately above the shoal, and everything depends upon careful observation.

There is, however, another kind of lure fishing that must be considered, and that is deep fishing with spoon or feathers. Mackerel are taken on the old-fashioned and very simple mackerel spinner which can be obtained in any tackle shop. The spinner or the single feather fly is fished as deeply as need be by putting on a large lead weight which is generally conical in shape. This heavy weight guarantees that the line, however stout, will twist and kink even with the largest brass swivels and so an anti-kink device is fashioned from something suitable, such as an old toothbrush handle.

The catching of mackerel with this kind of tackle may have novelty and a little excitement when the fish are hauled up, but there is very little 'feel' to the business. Often the fisherman is in doubt as to whether or not the mackerel is on the hook.

The same applies to deep spinning which is occasionally varied by dropping the line overboard from an anchored boat and making an almost vertical retrieve. The real art of sea-fishing is something much more refined and spinning or fly-fishing is a technique best employed in shallow water or where fish are close to the surface.

Lures originated in the dim past, perhaps on occasions when bait was unob-tainable or when some highly inventive fisherman decided to experiment, having seen how fish attacked others of their kind.

Even the pike has been taken on a fly. Such things as pike flies are mentioned in fishing books even if they are rarely resorted to by the pike fishermen. A pike fly, with its feathers and fur washed firmly along the shank of the hook is, of course, simply another imitation fish. All feathered lures take on a different shape once they are completely saturated and sink. Every lure or spoon must therefore be fished with some conception of its shape and its appearance to the fish. Without this feeling for the business of spinning or lure fishing everything depends on luck and the rewards will be small. This applies to fishing in fresh water or in the sea, with a small trout fly or the biggest salmon fly. The angler must fish with this constantly in mind, as well as confidence that, in the very next second, a fish will take!

4

Baits and Their Uses

Bait fishing is undoubtedly the most productive way of catching fish with a rod and line, for there is no more certain way of getting a fish to take than by offering it the thing it most enjoys. There are drawbacks, however, and some of them cannot be overcome.

Fish feed on things which are temporarily plentiful, things that may be small, too small to be of any use to the angler baiting a hook, things which may be hard, and again unsuitable for the hook. Bream who love the muds of sluggish waters, and trout who only survive in well-oxygenated lakes and streams, both feed upon the larvae of mosquitoes. Mosquitoes have been stimulated to breed in warm weather. The larvae are there, long afterwards, hatching and wriggling out of the silt, threadlike, twisting and squirming little blood-red worms.

No one could put such a small thing on the finest hooks ever made, and if one could, the little red worm would die. It would no longer wriggle and squirm. The bream or the trout would go for one that did.

There are scores of instances of this barrier between the angler's ability to fool fish and the natural feeding habit of a carp or bream which could lead to its capture. The business of bait fishing is to a large extent one of compromise. In a way it is fortunate that this is so. Complete success on the angler's part would have eliminated all the kinds of fish he could eat and made others scarce or very wary.

Given that a fish eating minute things which can't be used as bait turn and take a good fat worm, the proper study of fish of every species is to see that the bait offered is attractive. In the case of natural things it must look natural.

A boiled potato, a bread crust, a moulded knob of cheese may be outside this study. In the case of pastes and other 'manufactured' baits there is something to be said later on the way they are presented.

The commoner natural baits of the coarse fisherman are worms and maggots. The former may be as big garden worms known as lobs, or the small midden worm streaked with red and with a certain flavour of compost about it. The latter will be the lusty bluebottle maggot in his natural state, milk-fed, toughened off in bran, and full of life. Or it may be his counterpart, dyed to suit the foible of the angler who wouldn't dream of offering a natural maggot to the chub or chavender, but one coloured red, bright orange, or yellow.

MAGGOTS

The maggot is all things to the fish it is offered to, for there is small chance of the bluebottle maggot falling into the river. The maggot feeds in carrion meat – the carcass of a dead animal. It isn't a natural inhabitant of the water, but there are all kinds of larval insects which the bluebottle maggot resembles that either fall into the water or emerge from the muds. The maggot is easily fastened to the hook. It will stay alive, twisting and jerking for a long time. It is this movement, more than anything else, that makes the maggot one of the most useful baits ever devised by man.

A live maggot is sometimes added to a trout fly. Anyone who has used it in this way knows how much better his chances become, although the purist fly-fisherman will have none of it.

The maggot also serves as the most useful ground bait. It draws feeding fish to the angler's swim although it takes some judgement to know how much ground-baiting needs to be done, for there is such a thing as overdoing it. One maggot on a hook could be overlooked by fish rooting among a thousand or more!

Grow your own maggots if you must, but it is a business that may bring trouble on your head in hot weather. A piece of old meat crawling with suet-like maggots advertises itself. Only anglers delight in such a sight. It is better to buy your supplies from a tackle dealer who will have a weekly order with the maggot factory. Maggot production is big business.

The expert breeds only the biggest and best and he dyes them to suit demand. Once you have your supply you may use them, or keep them (if the weather is not too hot) in a suitable place until you are able to go fishing. A good place to keep the maggot can is in a cool drain, provided the drain isn't in danger of filling up. The refrigerator at home is almost certain to be reserved for more wholesome things than your tin of maggots which, by the way, needs to have a perforated lid to allow them to breathe.

Kept in a warm place maggots continue to develop, pass through the chrysalis stage, and finally hatch into fine bluebottles which, alas, are not very much use to the fisherman.

The worm ranks with the maggot in its usefulness. It is bigger, more obvious, and sometimes much more active. It, too, needs to be toughened or hardened off, even if it can be used freshly-dug from the garden.

There are different ways of hardening worms. One of the simplest is to keep them for several days in a can of moss. This results in the worms casting earth they have swallowed and becoming tougher, more durable when on the hook. A soft worm is soon broken up and removed by a fish or a shoal of small fishes. Hardening off the worm is as important as fishing it on the bottom.

While you may even buy your worms (there are firms that advertise lob-worms at so much a dozen) just as you can buy the maggots you need, you will probably want to dig them from your garden. Worms aren't always plentiful, however, and they are often difficult to find.

It is wise to cultivate worms. This can be done by ensuring that a particular plot of ground retains its moisture and has a good proportion of vegetable matter in the soil. A compost heap may be most productive but worms need soil. Too often the compost heap consists of liquefying vegetable leaves and stalks, becoming a heavy mass of stuff that is much too hot to allow worms to breed. The worm patch should be forked over, fed with a certain amount of vegetable matter, and covered with an old sack or two to ensure the soil remaining moist. Worms will rise to the surface and be easily forked out when you are planning to go fishing in a day or two.

Worming is a method that lends itself to a number of fishing techniques. In trout fishing the worm may be ledgered, used with or without a weight, or fished upstream and allowed to trundle back on the current. In this and other sorts of fishing it may be long-trotted, that is, allowed to float gently on the current and steered along by the angler on the bank who tries to cover all the likely swims in the process.

The cynic talks of fishing as a business involving a worm at one end of the line and a fool at the other, but worm fishing is an art. Few fish lie waiting for the first mouthful that splashes down in front of their noses. The worm must arrive on the scene as a worm washed out of the earth of the bank or carried on the current arrives. It will be allowed to lie, twisting and wriggling perhaps, for a minute or two, or minutes on end even, when the fish sees it drift into view. It may be scooped up greedily or nudged and prodded by more than one fish before it is whisked away. The weight lifts or the float up above dips and the message arrives at the rod. The fisherman lifts his hand. The hook is fixed and the worm has done what it was intended to do.

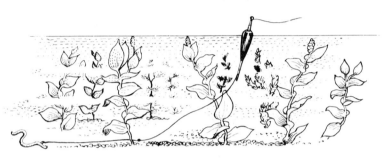

LIGHT FLOAT

This, of course, is not always the case. The worm may fall through coloured and cloudy water and lie on silt. There may not be a fish in sight. The angler has anchored the worm in place by fine shot, or a sizeable lead where the river flows strongly. He studies the way his line is out, the position of his bait, the drag on his float if he is using one: all this after having plumbed depth to know how far down the mud or gravel bed is. Now he must be like the heron and study to be patient.

The flavour of that worm is carried in the water. The fish that is searching for food may come across it in the course of its journey upstream. He may track it down like a dog on the scent of a rabbit.

This particular aspect of bank fishing has less appeal to the imagination than fishing a worm through the minor rapids of a fast river. It can sometimes remove the angler from the true art of deceiving a fish by the use of rod and line. A worm that lies on the bottom waiting to be discovered may be fastened to a line that is cast from a rod or to one that is simply pegged on the bank and to which the 'fisherman' returns on the following day, whether this is legal or not.

Ground-baiting with cloud bait, maggots, chopped worms or any other thing likely to attract fish elevates the use of the worm as bait and is to be recommended.

Apart from worms and maggots used in coarse and game fishing, there are a few natural baits to which the angler occasionally resorts such as caterpillars, dock grubs (they look like outsize maggots but are not so easily come by) and even grasshoppers.

Neither grasshoppers nor caterpillars are very easily put on hooks. Living flies are sometimes used on hooks specially designed to hold them by the wings but delicate baits are generally not worth the trouble.

CATERPILLAR

A thing like a woodlouse or slater may be put on a hook and dropped in front of a trout. I have caught trout with them, but only after 'feeding' the fish for something like an hour until the trout got the taste of them and became used to them washing down through the pool.

There remains the branch of fishing where baits are most important of all – fishing in the sea. So few of the fish that may be caught in salt water take spinners, and so many of them feed on the bottom, that bait fishing holds the answer to success in salt water, and the baits are more numerous. The mullet, which is an extremely wary fish and quick to take itself away, may be fed on the tide with a variety of things such as bread, bits of bacon fat or small cubes of meat cooked or uncooked and so lulled that the morsel slipping down among the rest but concealing a hook is bolted before the mullet knows what it is all about. This is something akin to ground baiting in the river.

In deep water the angler drops a bag of offal, chicken guts or some other material with a flavour attractive to scavenging fish, over the side of the boat. In a while he may expect to gather a company of inquisitive fish of different kinds. While the bag is down sending out its essences, the fisherman's chosen bait is down too, laid out on the bottom or dangling from a paternoster.

The fish of deep water is far less suspicious of strange objects than the fish of the river who is frightened time and time again. The sea fish is always competing with others of his own kind who will rush in to snap up whatever is there to be taken. Ground baiting in the manner employed on the river or canal would be quite useless in the sea, even in the best fishing places, because currents would soon carry off the bait scattered from the boat even if fish didn't clear it all up before it reached the seabed.

The commoner baits of the sea angler are two kinds of worm dug on the shore, the lugworm and the much more useful rag which can be had after strenuous digging in comparatively hard ground.

The lugworm lives in the sand. As the tides run back it retreats into its burrow, casting the sand it has swallowed and leaving the rope of it on the surface in one spot and a few inches away leaving a roundel mark to show where its head finally slid beneath the surface.

LUGWORM

The wonderful thing about the lugworm is its ability to dive once the man with the fork or spade alarms it. There isn't a bait digger who hasn't pursued the lugworm into a water quagmire and lost it. The expert worm-digger looks at the line of the cast, and the breathing mark, and knows that immediately below the lugworm is comfortably lying in fairly solid sand.

Because a spade always compacts sand and leaves a cavity into which water soon flows, the bait-digger cuts a short trench, no more than three or four spadefuls alongside the 'lie' of the hidden lugworm. He then loses no time but turns and digs down to remove a spit of sand (which should hold the worm) and spreads the spadeful on the undug surface in front of his trench.

The best lugworm is the one that comes intact from the sand and can be 'stripped' – its 'meal' of sand and other body liquids squeezed out before it is stored in dry newspaper for that day's fishing.

There are anglers who prefer to use a fork for digging lugworm and there is sometimes a lot to be said for turning over a densely populated lugworm bed,

A south-east bait digger shows the tell-tale signs to look for when digging for lugworm

(*South East Angling and Photographic Services*)

but the spade is a thing that complies with the old fisherman's maxim that catching one at a time is good enough.

While the lugworm will serve for most fish, there is no doubt that the rag is a worm much to be preferred for bass and most of the bigger fish. The rag is unaccommodating, however. It doesn't protect itself by shooting back into the almost liquid sand down below. It lives in the grit and shingle, isolated from too many others of its kind by buried boulders and rocks which greatly hinder its being excavated.

A good ragworm is worth twice or three times as many lugworms, but few anglers dig a bucketful between tides as they may comfortably do when getting lugworm on the right sand strip. More like a centipede than a worm, the rag can actually inflict a nip to the fingers of the man who picks it up.

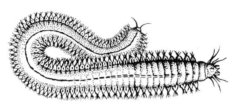

RAGWORM

The angler who has ragworm as bait fishes more confidently than one who makes do with lugworm or resorts to mussels or limpets, neither of which rate very much higher than the packeted 'salted' and dried lugworms bought from the tackle shop.

Almost as good a bait in some places as any sort of worm is the 'soft' or peeler crab, as it is more properly called. Like the prawn, the peeler crab is to be found

PRAWN

in and around the weedy pools where the tide stops. It is, in fact, a crab in the process of changing its protective shell. Fish love to come across these defenceless crabs when they shoal through the pools.

The squid and the razor fish are most useful baits on occasions too.

Finally we come to fish themselves. Small fish make up a great part of the diet of predators that rarely come into the shallows, fish like the tope and the dogfish.

For the tope, a whiting of just the right size produces action when the shark-like tope snaps it up and tightens the line. What more can an angler ask than for his rod to bend almost to breaking point and the reel spin until the oil in its bearings begins to smoke?

Sometimes there is no holding the tope, but he is a fish that isn't always there. He travels from one place to another in summer and he is generally taken from a boat, although sizeable specimens have been taken fishing from the beach. For such a fish a gaff is needed. He can straighten all but the heavy forged hook that swivels at the end of a wire trace and, like the dogs (spurred and spotted dogfish), he may scavenge in company, one following close upon another.

There are a number of fish that scavenge like the lesser sharks and can sometimes be taken on the guts of a chicken or rabbit when nothing better is at hand. But it pays to give the fish, whether it is a big grey mullet, or policeman-like bass, the thing it feeds upon when it comes to the shore or into the estuary.

5

Tackles and Knot-Tying

½ BLOOD KNOT

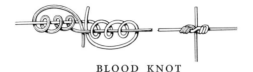

BLOOD KNOT

Always make sure that your equipment includes such things as a really sharp knife, a clean rag, a pair of pliers, a pair of scissors, a disgorger, a gag if you are fishing for pike, a small sharpening stone for putting a new edge on a blunted hook, a priest for making an end of the fish. Be prepared for disasters and there won't be disasters!

The way you set up the tackle holds the secret of success in fishing. It is not really enough to be in the right place at the right time. Even if the first fish that comes along is one that never saw a baited hook before, you are not the first fisherman. Generations of fish, hunted by generations of anglers, have acquired a protective instinct against things that are not quite natural.

There are other reasons why a study of the way to rig up or lay out your tackle pays dividends. Without some degree of care you will often lose expensive tackle. Without knowing how to overcome obstacles you may find yourself with tackle and no bait, or even worse, bait and all your tackle lost.

What you must learn is how to make your tackle secure and how to rig it up in certain instances, so that if you lose anything it is a small loss and something can be quickly replaced.

There are other considerations, of course, some of them depending upon plain common sense.

How, for instance, does a prawn or a shrimp move through the water? Anyone who has watched a shrimp in a pool has seen it jerk its way – backwards. If you put a prawn or a shrimp on your tackle the wrong way round it will appear to be moving in a very strange way when a not so hungry fish glides along to inspect it.

If you cast a worm into a streamy run and it lies out there, anchored by too much lead, it will be conspicuous and have very little chance of coming to the attention of a fish if the current is sweeping heavier objects downstream. Big fish may move up through the flood but they don't stay there to pick up food.

If you fish in the sea from a rocky headland the chances are that your weight may get caught in a crevice in the rocks and you will lose not only the weight but the tackle above it, a paternoster, a float, the hooks and the bait.

It is a tiring job digging bait and bait is expensive to buy, even if you have all the hooks and swivels and floats you may ever need. An extravagant outlook will soon bring all your labour to nothing. The simple way is to attach your weight to the tackle by a length of nylon of lower breaking strain than the main fishing line, so that you lose only the lead. At the same time you may use bits of old lead pipe or even items of old iron in such circumstances, and not the 'shop-bought' leads you might choose for a sandy beach.

While the common sense of angling will soon convince you that you must take precautions to see that you don't lose valuable items, you will need to learn from the outset that sound knots, knots that won't unravel or slip or cause the line to snap, are as important as having a sound rod.

It is galling to discover that a fish just about to be gaffed or brought to the net

A change of fly
(*Ken Whitehead*)

suddenly turns and swirls in the water with your line trailing from the side of its mouth, a knot having slipped. It is equally frustrating to haul up your line and discover that although you had a good tug the bait is intact and the fish is never hooked. Why should this be, if you have rigged up the ledger tackle to let the fish have enough movement and time to lift the bait and carry it? A trout rises once of its own free will to take a natural insect on the surface of the lake. You cast to him. He obliges by turning and snapping up the artificial fly and the line is suddenly slack, the fly on the end of your line is in the fish's mouth. The knot has slipped. Try as you may you won't persuade that good trout to have another hook in his mouth for quite some time, perhaps even a day or two.

Beginners will sometimes lose not only the fly but the cast, not only the lead weight on the sealine, but everything including the wire trace and the swivel. The weak point is at the knot attaching wire trace and swivel to the nylon line. So you must learn the knots to use all the way down from the reel line to the weight, from the floating line to the cast, and finally the fly.

Perhaps the most useful knot any angler can know is the blood knot, the whole blood knot and the half-blood knot. With the whole blood knot one may join the line of equal diameter and also make a dropper to which a second or third hook may be attached.

The half-blood knot is the one by which all swivels can be securely fastened and spoons or spinners be reliably put on the trace. Bear in mind that the weakest point in any line is where the knot is. Take time and make sure that you tie secure knots. It will make all the difference to your enjoyment. Nothing in fishing should ever be done in a hurry or be slipshod.

Once, having rigged up a tackle for a would-be pike fisherman, I left him to attach the already baited line to the reel line. An hour or so later I was asked to come and see the strange sight of two pike floats bobbing away out towards the reeds on the far side of the small lake. The floats had never gone under, but the pike had taken the bait. The final knot had been a slipshod affair. At the first movement of the fish the line had parted. Fortunately the rest of the tackle was sound and believe it or not, the pike floats were 'snagged' with a spinner and the fish played and brought to the gaff in spite of everything! A good blood knot was all that was needed.

In another case, fishing from a waterlogged punt, a companion and I took pike, one of which, as it was about to be swung inboard, fell off the line with the spinner still in its mouth. The knot hadn't been a good one. The angry pike swam up and down in the punt snapping at the feet of his captors for quite a time before he was gaffed!

The big one that got away isn't really the story in a lot of cases. The real story is one of bad tackle or bad knot-tying. Let us consider the knots for fly-fishing in particular, for they are few and quite simple. How to attach the line to the cast? The cast is loop-ended. It comes that way. Making a loop is simple but it is illustrated for the benefit of the beginner. The fly line is attached in one of two ways and a simple illustration below shows how this may be done.

KNOTTING CAST TO LINE

The blood knot, which is used in every branch of fishing either for making a joint in a line or fashioning droppers, is not too difficult to learn. The half-blood is what its name suggests but can only be tied to the end of a swivel or to a metal loop. Both kinds of blood knot must be pulled up very tightly and tested before they are used, but remember, of course, no line will stand a strain beyond its rating!

The half-blood may sometimes be used to attach very large flies to a line. The full blood knot, with one end untrimmed, forms a dropper on a cast but tying the average kind of fly (salmon or trout) to the cast cannot be done better than with the turle knot as illustrated.

HOOK TO CAST

Experienced anglers swear by other knots, but the foregoing will serve the beginner until he finds need of others. It is possible to add droppers to a cast, for instance, with a simple running hitch: but sliding knots have their disadvantages and I have always found it better to take time and do without the 'benefits' of improvisation.

With the knots all tied securely in a fishermanlike fashion there remains the question of the great variety of tackles to be used in fishing either in rivers and lakes or the sea. Some of these will call for floats, some of quill, some self-cocking, some sliding, some large, some small. In the case of floats the ultimate choice will depend upon the water to be fished and species of fish being fished for. Some of the types of float are illustrated here, but they must be chosen to suit the water.

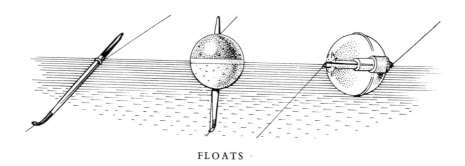

FLOATS

In certain circumstances, especially when fishing in the shade, at dusk or in coloured or turbulent water, it will be found that 'day-glow' floats are more readily seen by the angler, but here again the use of such things depends upon the circumstances and the species of fish.

A fine light float is needed for roach because roach are shy and keen-sighted; but you will want a substantial float to carry a pike line since it has to act as a support for a bait of some size or hold the line clear of things which might become a hazard when the fish makes his run. The bubble float is a device to enable the angler to fish beyond the reach of the ordinary fly rod. It is generally frowned upon by devoted fly-fishermen although it has its uses (in a larger size) in fishing in the sea, where it may control a drifted prawn or hold a bait for a wrasse on the edge of rocks where he feeds.

Sea floats in general need to be a little more conspicuous than the floats used by the coarse fisherman; but match-fishing floats may sometimes be no more than the most delicate quill if the angler is relying upon making weight with a great catch of very small fish.

To make a prawn tackle the do-it-yourself fisherman (which a great many fishermen are compelled to become since even small items of tackle can be very costly) takes a fairly stiff stainless steel wire and fashions a loop on it curling it round one of the hooks of a treble. The tackle is as illustrated.

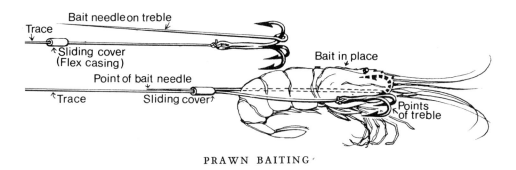

PRAWN BAITING

There are a number of variations on this tackle, some employing a sizeable sewing needle fastened through the eye to the bend in the treble by means of fine stainless steel wire, but sewing needles tend to rust if put away before they are dry. Alternatively, a baiting needle may be used and the trace or cast brought through the body of the prawn and tied to the hook which is then drawn up until it is among the prawn's 'whiskers'. This will serve so long as your prawn remains intact. It is a time-consuming thing to have to bait up in this way, however, hence the ready-made tackles generally used.

Ledgering, where there is no problem of the weight being sucked along by the tide, and the tackle ceasing to be what it was laid out to be, may be rigged up with a lead known as an Arlesley bomb. This is a symmetrical, pear-drop lead in the top of which is moulded a swivel. The beauty of such a lead is that it doesn't easily snag up on the bottom. It can be lifted cleanly and smoothly. It is ideal for ledgering where the tackle is in no danger of being moved by heavy waves or fluctuations in the current. In such cases and where a paternoster is used the angler will almost certainly want a type of lead that actually beds down or takes hold on the bottom.

Stops on ledgers are achieved by several methods. In some cases all the angler does is to insert a piece of stout nylon or bristle crosswise on the running line. This will be all that is needed until the line runs as the fish draws it through the swivel on the weight.

The movement of the fish may be indicated by the turning of the reel handle or, if a second swivel is put on the line above the ledger weight the final lift of the weight tells the fisherman that something worth stopping is making off with the bait.

Sometimes a larger swivel is incorporated in the line to act as a stop when it comes up against the weight. There are many refinements in sea fishing, including wire runners from which the ledger weight is suspended; but the more elaborate the rig the more chances there are of things becoming tangled up, especially in water that is turbulent.

The cheese 'bite indicator', mentioned for bottom fishing for coarse fish such as chub, is illustrated as a guide to the method. There are variations of this with small twists of silver paper or pieces of ordinary paper clipped to the line so that an angler may see at a glance what is happening to his offering.

A kind of sea fishing that comes within the scope of tackling up but isn't done with rod and line in the conventional way is rafting or, to use an older word, ottering.

While the use of an otter is illegal on lakes or rivers, the principle can well be used in the sea. A keel-shaped heavy board is weighted along its lower edge and rigged up with three cords like a kite. The weighting is done so that the board sinks deeper into the water at one end than at the other. This causes the 'water kite', when it carries a fishing line attached to its rigging, to catch the wind and angle its way out in the current.

The number of hooks that are baited or dressed with 'flies' is a matter for experiment but the result is that a set of baits or lures is worked out over a likely bay or down an estuary. If the fisherman is lucky enough to intercept a shoal he needs to have made sure his line is strong enough to let him haul back his wooden kite when two or three fish are struggling at the end of the droppers.

Rafting is also done with a straightforward board with a small mast and sail. Again, a really stout line or even a rope may be needed to enable the angler to drag back his catch if and when his baits are taken. The beauty of this method is that the droppers can be made long or short and the bait kept down with small leads so that fish well below the surface can have their chance.

Neither the raft nor the otter can be used in rough weather but the angler who hasn't a boat and knows a likely fishing mark can sometimes get fish where he otherwise couldn't hope to reach them. Greed, however, will be the undoing of the angler who tries to catch too many at one time. Once fish are dead on the end of a device the tide won't allow the fisherman to retrieve, gulls and other predators quickly take their toll.

Another device which the angler who comes without his rod may adopt is the bottle caster. This is simply a handline and baited tackle carefully wound on to a good sized wine bottle. The bottle is firmly held by the base and a cast made by jerking the neck of the bottle in the direction the fisherman wants his bait to go. The line 'unspools' as the weight and the bait draw it from the bottle's neck. Once the line is out, of course, the fisherman is handlining, but generally handlining farther out than he could reach by ordinary means.

This 'bottle fishing' was popular off the Australian beaches before the fixed-spool reel was used for sea-fishing. Many sea anglers have tried to get line out by similar devices including coiled springs and crossbows. One man was highly successful in using a clockwork boat to trail his line where fish were feeding. He, however, ended up in court, charged with poaching, because his toy boat sailed across a trout lake where bailiffs became interested in a grown man who spent so much of his time 'playing' like a small boy.

6

Coarse Fish: Predators — Pike and Perch

It is undoubtedly true that there are not as many pike as there were in the past. This is true of many species in different places for the simple reason that today there are more anglers, and cars make every good fishing place more accessible than it was.

The pike remains widely distributed and it is found in the Norfolk Broads, many lakes in England and Wales, lochs in Scotland and Ireland, as well as in some ponds, meres, old canals, stocked gravel pits, rivers and their feeder streams. It is not generally numerous in any particular place except when fish become gregarious at spawning time.

Since the pike lives to a large extent upon other fish of whatever species the water supports – dace, rudd, roach, minnows, trout – it can best be caught with live bait.

You can set up a rod and have a nice day catching the bait before pike fishing. Small perch will do, if there are no dace or minnows, despite the belief that the perch's dorsal fin puts the pike off taking him when offered as a bait.

Live-baiting is frowned upon by a lot of pike specialists and there are debates as to whether the biggest pike will be taken on a spoon or on natural bait. Natural bait will almost certainly win in the end and live bait is so obviously more attractive.

Your rod will be almost any stout two or three piece rod strong enough to bring in a twenty or thirty pounder (if you are lucky!) and the reel will be either the fixed spool or multiplier. In the case of the former, make sure that the line isn't less than it finally takes to hold the pike at the moment of gaffing, say about ten pounds breaking-strain. This will mean that you won't try to gaff the fish out until he has had his fight and second run.

Tackle up for live-baiting by hooking your small fish in the upper lip. Make sure that the hook is right through the lip. Use paternoster tackle as illustrated and a weight sufficient to hold the bottom against any slight current that may be running. Remember the pike will not be dallying in fast water!

The line is supported on the surface by two floats or 'bungs'. These should be coloured orange or red so that they can be seen if the water is weedy or the light is bad. The purpose of the two bungs is to enable you to strike your fish at exactly the right moment. A pike takes a fish *across* its body, turns it in his jaws and then swallows it *head* first. The purpose of the two floats is to indicate what is happening.

As the pike takes your tethered dace or minnow he will move a short distance. The weight will drag on the bottom and the first bung will almost certainly sink. To lift the rod now would be to start a tug-of-war with your pike *without the hook being inside his jaws*. Wait, holding the rod and getting ready for the run which will follow the strike, *until the second bung has gone down*. Now the pike is gorging the fish. Lift the rod and keep the line under tension.

A fine haul of pike; the smaller ones make good eating

(*Ken Whitehead*)

The hook will be driven home. The pike, discovering he is tethered, will rush off into the deeps. Your line will cut water. The bungs will rip on through weed and perhaps through obstructions under water but they will slip along the line under pressure and generally not cause you too much trouble.

Let the pike run, exerting only a slight pressure, either by adjusting drag on your reel or by keeping finger-control on the reel spool. When he has finished his first run he will let you recover line, but as he nears the bank he will almost certainly become alarmed again and make a second dash.

Most pike give up after this second run, but there are big ones who continue to fight, going round in circles, swirling and splashing, particularly if the gaff is waved above them! Take time, make sure, and gaff the fish out as smoothly as you can without injuring him. Put him back if you want to catch pike again, or have any thought for anyone else who might want to.

Dead baits need not be hooked with the same care and sometimes a treble rather than an ordinary single hook (which is best when the bait is alive) will be used to secure the dead bait. The bait doesn't need to be suspended on a paternoster. It can be laid out with a running ledger or a simple arrangement that keeps the bait in the swim and lying on the bottom where the pike will eventually discover it.

The line may again be supported with two bungs and the strike handled as before.

You will find that rudd are better dead bait than perch, perhaps because of their flavour or their colour which is brighter than that of any perch. Dace are better than either of these, but the pike may also be tempted with herring, a fish he isn't likely to come across even in the most brackish of the Broads of East Anglia.

Another way of handling dead bait is to rig it on to a spinning flight, consisting of a bait needle equipped with spinning vanes and a set of hooks (two trebles), fixed into the body of the dead fish or lashed to its back and flanks with nylon. The spun bait is offered on a soft but strong steel trace, as the ordinary dead bait sometimes will be, because a pike can quickly cut a single nylon trace. It is cast and retrieved with attention to the habits of pike and the way an injured or very sick fish might behave as it struggles along the bottom gasping its last, with a dash, a twitch, a pause and then another convulsive movement. This is what makes the pike take, and nothing looks better to him than a real fish.

The time to fish? Well, there are more pike about in summer and they can be taken with the spinner without much trouble. You can use an Abu spoon three inches in length or a Mepps. Both sorts are used on a wire trace with two swivels. The smaller spinner is sometimes weighted to keep it down, although this is more essential in winter than in summer.

Pike fishing at its very best is winter fishing. It is a much colder business and there aren't minnows in the shallows to be trapped, so that you must make arrangements to catch rudd or dace (which you will learn how to catch in due course).

The big pike moves infrequently. A tasty rudd is what he is looking for in the lake, or dace in the river. Fish for him with patience if you really hope to catch a big one. The records to date are in some confusion and you will be nowhere near a record-breaker unless you catch one over forty pounds.

Gaffing a pike through the lower jaw is the best method
(*Ken Whitehead*)

The legends and the relics of pike caught in the past indicate that there may have been one or two pike of seventy pounds or more in the wild lochs of the North or in Irish waters. A gamekeeper is supposed to have brought the Loch Ken pike home on his back, its head at his shoulder and its tail trailing on the ground!

The pike you catch is hardly likely to be such a monster, but remember, if you have seen a pike of five pounds in the weeds of the canal there is almost sure to be one half as big again not very far off. If you have seen one of ten pounds there may be one of twenty. If you see a twenty pounder then a thirty pounder isn't too big to dream about.

The biggest pike will be found where food is plentiful. A great many pike fishing enthusiasts look for a giant from Loch Lomond in Scotland. Some have hopes of finding a monster in a weeded wilderness, perhaps the stew-pond of some derelict mansion.

Pike fishing has the glamour and mystery of the Loch Ness monster itself. Who knows what lives in the clearing out beyond the weeds where the old boathouse slumps in mossy ruins and small fish splash and splutter out of the water? There could lie your monster pike!

Finally, it is possible to preserve bait and use them in winter or when conditions prevent your getting freshly-caught baits, but nothing that is preserved ever has the same flavour as the fresh natural bait. Let preserved bait be the last resort. It is possible to use traces of woven nylon instead of annealed steel wire and there is much to be said for this because the softness of nylon allows the bait to move with a more natural flexibility.

You may troll your dead bait or spinner behind a boat. Some people do, but it means trusting to luck rather than studying the places in which a pike likes to lie, and this isn't fishing with imagination. Only troll if you can find nothing better to do! It isn't really fishing for any particular fish or even species of fish.

And the pike fly? Pig's wool for the body, glass beads for the eyes, wings of the peacock eye fibres and tail of any colourful long hackles. It will work, but not many people have caught a big pike on it, or it would have been talked about!

The perch, like the pike, is a predatory and aggressive fish. It will never be found much bigger than the average jack pike. It follows that everything must be scaled down in size when considering ways and means of catching a good perch, for the very big spoon isn't going to catch very big perch. A good-sized herring will make the perch head the other way. He too will take a fly among other things.

The problem is often how to avoid catching lesser perch and only lay the tackle out for the big one.

How big is a big perch? Between two-and-a-half and three pounds would satisfy the most ambitious perch fisherman! The record runs well over four

The perch is armed with an outsized dorsal fin

(*Ken Whitehead*)

pounds but again there are accounts of unauthenticated perch of twice this weight.

The best bait for the really big perch is the lobworm. Since the shallows in summer are almost invariably the haunts of shoals, the place to fish for the bigger fish is in the deeper water of the lake. Here you may choose to float fish in the conventional way, having used a weight to plumb the depth.

Unlike the pike, the perch's eyes are on the side of his skull like the eyes of many other fish that feed on the bottom and in midwater. The perch looks right and left and up and down. Often he inclines to study the bottom more thoroughly and discovers the lobworm wriggling into the gravel or disturbing the silt.

The first inclination you will have of his interest will be the gentle bob of the float or, if you are ledgering, a drift away of line accompanied by the slightest revolution of the bale arm of your fixed-spool reel. At this, collect your wits!

The bobbing float is characteristic in fishing worm for perch. Although he is a large-mouthed and greedy-looking fish, the perch doesn't behave like the hungry pike. He nibbles once or twice and sometimes expels the worm from his mouth when he feels the hook. He will even do this with a worm that has no hook in it.

PERCH

I once kept perch in a large tank and watched tugs at the bait making the float bob. The perch may actually have backed off each time before his final rush. This is followed by the float slanting in the water and going on down out of sight. Now is the time to strike and drive the hook home.

A perch of a pound will fight harder than a jack pike of four pounds. When he comes to the net you will see that he has more of anger than anything else in his expression, while a pike simply looks baleful and menacing. You haven't got your perch until you have him in the keep net. He fights and jerks until the last minute.

Fishing with lobworm calls for the same size of hook (a No. 6) as fishing with minnow, which is as good a way of getting perch in summer as any. Minnow fishing for perch is also a shade more refined than using live or dead bait for pike.

One of the simplest ways is to thread the nylon attached to the hook in through the mouth of the dead minnow and out through the body, having weighted the hook shank with lead shot of a suitable size to keep the bait well down in the water. The dead minnow is worked in the sink-and-draw technique. That is, it is allowed to sink after being cast and is then recovered in jerks at intervals long enough to allow a perch in mid-water to drop down or rise and follow it. The take will make you think that you have snagged something but a moment later you will feel the drag on your reel. The rod will vibrate in your hand. The minnow is now deep in the gullet of the perch and the perch is on his way.

A line of three to three-and-a-half pounds breaking strain is enough to cope with any kind of perch. Should a record perch take the bait the spool slips. Even a ten pound pike couldn't tighten the line enough to make it break.

Bring the fish in carefully and without being heavy-handed. Perch are not often lightly hooked but the business of fishing really should be to cultivate delicacy. A hooked fish should not be handled roughly. Lift the fish out after you have brought him over the net which you have already submerged in the water. Hold him gently. Use the disgorger to get the hook out of his mouth. If he is deeply hooked and it is obvious that removing the hook will cause the fish pain then kill him quickly, knocking him on the head with a stone or, better still, with a 'priest' bought specially for the purpose.

You will get your lobworms, the smaller brandling and red-streaked worms from the garden or your specially cultivated 'wormery', but minnows will have to be caught. A useful minnow trap can be devised by unscrewing the lid of a Kilner jar and dispensing with the glass. An open-ended cone to fit the top of the jar can be easily made from a piece of perforated zinc. This cone is inserted in place of the glass lid and afterwards held by the metal lid retainer. Attach a good length of cord to the jar, use bread for bait and leave the jar submerged in the shallows of the lake where minnow shoals are feeding. You will catch all the minnows you need for fishing for pike, perch, trout or chub.

MINNOWS

Alternatively, the tackle dealer may sell you a minnow trap, and a bait can be designed to keep the minnows alive until you need them.

Apart from worming and the sink-and-draw minnow, perch may be caught by spinning and by fly-fishing. A light spinning rod is needed. A heavy one isn't necessary and isn't really flexible enough to cast the small spinner. Almost any spoon of about an inch in length will attract perch, although more often than not the sort of fish that take most readily are those small shoaling perch that haunt shallows where minnows and small fry are plentiful. There is, however, always the chance that a good perch may come to investigate the spinner, although the bigger fish are distinctly solitary in their habits.

If there are other species of fish in the lake the small spinner may result in some variety in your catch, as the case may be if you fish fly. Use the trout rod and line recommended for fly-fishing.

The best flies are flashy and gaudy ones – lures such as the Butcher, which carries a red tag and has a silver body to go with a black hackle and the blue feather of the mallard's wing. The Zulu, a fly closely related to the Butcher, is another useful lure for perch. I have actually taken rudd on both. In the main, however, perch that take spoons or lures are rarely more than the very average fish for the water.

Nothing quite equals bait-fishing, with live bait, dead bait or worm. The finesse of ledger-fishing, the sporadic excitement of float fishing, the thrill when sink-and-draw pays off excels that of all other methods. Even a spinning enthusiast may sometimes admit that there is a grinding monotony about throwing out a spoon and winding it back again and again.

Perch fishing is disdainfully called small boys' fishing. If it is, it is surprising how many small boys of all ages there are in the angling world.

7

Coarse Fish: Shy Roach, Less Shy Rudd

While the pike and perch are the hawks of the fresh-water world, then the roach is among the doves. The shy roach is one of the most inconspicuous of fish. This is its habit, even when it isn't living in the coloured waters of some old canal, or sifting weed for morsels drifting down from where cattle stand drinking and swishing their tails.

Even in the gravelly reservoir, where the weed is more wholesome, or in the chalk stream quite free from pollution, it is not the way of the roach to swim boldly into the shallows as the shoaling perch does. Largely a bottom feeder, the roach feeds in the shallows in summer, and summer roaching has a special aura of peacefulness about it. The roach fisherman settles down to contemplate the water while all around him there is a drone of insects as dragonflies hover and dart above the rushes.

For such an angling delight to be yours you must find a sheltering tree or bush. This isn't to keep you out of the sun, but to hide you from roach passing through the swim or feeding right where you have dropped your baited hook.

The tackle for roach is as delicate and fine as any used by anglers. It calls for sensitive floats that cock with a small shot, gilt hooks no larger than No. 16 and bait of whatever kind you particularly fancy or regulations allow.

On some waters hemp is not permitted. On others ground baiting is forbidden. But ground baiting is generally an essential requirement if you are fishing with a float.

The bait that gives least trouble isn't always the one that takes most fish, but the maggot (one at a time for roach) is one of the most useful. You may, however, find your neighbour swearing by boiled wheat, paste or silkweed.

Remember above all that disturbing the water is the greatest deterrent to catching good roach. Float tackle accounts for more fish than ledgering, but this is not to say that the ledger isn't deadly when roach are on the gravel bottom of a reservoir. Where ground baiting isn't forbidden (it is not allowed on many Water Board fishing places) the roach fisherman has a good choice. He may throw in three or four of his maggots or some finely chopped worm. He may use paste made from bread and bran.

Baiting must not be overdone or it defeats its purpose. It must be put in with the same care as you cast your line and float. A big knob of paste making a plop and a set of widening rings on the surface will be enough to send your shy roach away. You might then just as well pick up everything and start somewhere else!

The rod you will use if you are setting out to become a dedicated roach fisherman will be one of suitable length for the rivers or reservoirs in your locality. The old Thames roach pole, for instance, was a very long one, but long rods, although they will reach over bushes and put the float down with accuracy, don't always handle well where bankside obstructions are close on either side.

Your rod, whatever its length, will be fairly stiff except at the tip, which will be flexible and responsive when you strike the fish. The roach you are most

Roach
(Ken Whitehead)

likely to catch will be around the half pound mark and a sensitive tip is necessary to strike most smaller fish. It will be made of hollow cane, Spanish reed, or it may be of fibre glass. The latter will stand up to your struggles when, instead of dropping the float in the right place, you have the misfortune to get it, and the line, among bushes overhanging the water.

To cast, having checked the depth with as little disturbance as possible, and fixed your quill float at the right distance from your baited hook (the lead no closer to the hook than twelve inches) you draw the line back in your hand without letting any more come off the reel, swing the rod and let the line run through the rings as you aim the float and bait to drop in the water. This is much easier said than done, and requires a little practice.

A fixed-spool reel makes casting easier but there is a certain delicacy and finesse in the use of the centre-pin that a good roach fisherman loves, and an ordinary centre-pin reel is quite uncomplicated.

So now the quill lies on the surface of the water. The bait sinks with the weight of the lead. Finally, when the float partially cocks, you are in business. There is nothing else to be done. You have baited your swim; the maggot is there on the small gilt hook. You are fishing near a weed bed or in the lea side of some small promontory. You must resist all temptation to lift the line out of the water too soon. A maggot doesn't drown so easily. If your paste was made properly it will stay on the hook!

The line you use will be no more than two pounds breaking strain. You can forget that the records include fish of three-and-a-half pounds or a little more. Most roach fishermen have to be content with much less. A fish of a pound is a good one, specially in summer.

You will feel the first movement in the rod perhaps, and then your heartbeat will quicken as the reel gives a slow partial revolution. All at once the cocked quill is missing. It has slipped sideways. A roach is on the line.

Almost instinctively you will raise the rod, stay the movement of the reel with your finger, and begin to draw the fish out of the swim if you can. This is often vital if you are to continue to fish a swim. Roach are so easily frightened away! You must get the net under your fish as deftly as you can. Don't splash. Don't hurry. Lift the landing net clear of the water. Swing it up to the bank and very gently take the fish out. Slip him into the keep net without making a disturbance or trampling the bank.

Take your time while you bait up. If you have managed everything without disturbance the fish will still be there, and if you haven't, haste on your part will be quite futile.

Now you have seen the roach. This is often the young fisherman's first close look at the fish. Few roach fisherman encourage a gallery of onlookers. Not many will risk spoiling the swim by allowing a boy to study what is in his keep net. You will see that the roach has a red eye. He is a most handsome fish with orange or yellow-red underbelly fins, a dark blue sheen to his back, silvery flanks and white underparts. His tail is often a sort of brownish olive. He will not be confused with the rudd if you note that his head is smaller and neater. Nor is the humped back quite so pronounced in the finer and less highly-coloured roach.

Summer roach are never quite so sullen as those caught in winter. They feed in the warm shallows in summer and the best sport is to be had either in the early morning or the late evening when swifts are black against the sky and it seems the world is settling down to doze.

In autumn the slow reaches of the winding river that roach love are often partly covered with falling leaves. These decomposing leaves seem to give the water a sour or bitter flavour, for roach never take in these circumstances. One simple rule must always be applied in roach fishing. When roach are on the feed they cannot be left to hook themselves.

Roach fishing may be a sort of contemplative man's recreation, but it should never be done casually. The float that slides away will rise and recock if you are not keeping your mind upon your business.

Baits for roach need to be studied in detail. Hemp fishermen swear by hemp. Users of paste have their secrets. There are those who would use nothing but maggot, or the worm on a ledger. Others try such things as elderberries. Silkweed will always be popular because this is one of the favourites of the feeding roach. Cloud bait attracts fish without giving them anything to eat and unless it is accompanied by your bait and perhaps a couple of maggots you mustn't expect roach to linger where there was nothing in the beginning.

To make cloud bait, first make rusks from bread baked in the oven and then pounded down so that you can scatter it on the water flowing through your chosen swim.

Paste is more a matter for the specialist because of the ingredients he considers necessary. An everyday paste for baiting a swim is made with bread and bran. Too much bran will feed the fish before you catch them. Too little bran will allow the bread to separate and flow in a sticky mess that does no good at all.

The stale bread must be thoroughly dried before it is finally soaked. This means drying in an oven until all moisture leaves it completely. It then needs to be ground down until no lumps remain. All the water must be squeezed out of it once it has been soaked again.

Bran added to soaked bread at this stage will give the mix a consistency that enables it to be formed into balls which must hold together, but flatten if you drop them on the floor. The mix must never be tacky, nor must it be kept and allowed to go sour.

Take the greatest care to keep the whole business clean. Remember that fish taste flavour in the water. If, for instance, bait is made up by someone with nicotine from smoking on his fingers the flavour is certain to contaminate the paste, and nicotine is a poison in any case!

If you are to use hemp then be sure it isn't boiled until it bursts but only simmered until the husk or shell of the seed begins to crack. Wheat may be 'scalded' in a bowl by pouring boiling water over it and leaving it to cool before straining the water off.

Some people use the water from simmered hemp in making paste bait. Others add a little aniseed which has great attraction. Small cubes of bread, the very smallest you can make to stay on the hook, will also serve as bait and crust dropped just beyond the flags may encourage roach to feed.

Bread crust itself makes a bait. Some people bottle and preserve elderberries and use them early in the following season. Roach will also take woodlouse or slater.

There are always experiments to be made in offering baits and all sorts of things that may be included in ground bait recipes – sugar, ground rice, a flavouring of cheese, a little custard powder. Silkweed can be gathered from wooden jetties, posts in the river, the timbers of the old boathouse or the beams and shuttering of the lock. There is nothing like giving the roach what it is feeding upon at a particular time.

Having called the roach the dove, it must be said that the rudd is much less delicate and less shy in his ways. He is, in fact, quite capable of dash at the trout fisherman's fly when a cast of flies is being fished towards the reeds from a boat. I have caught many rudd I didn't want doing just this.

The rudd haunts the sort of places in which young moorhen chicks take refuge in early summer – the fringe of the reeds and spaces between beds of weed. The roach may be caught by ledgering in such places and the rudd discriminates far less than the roach, being an altogether less highly-strung fish.

The same tactics as those used for roach are used against the rudd. The same degree of refinement may not be needed but the skilled angler takes a pride in doing everything with finesse.

Rudd, like roach, are fairly widely distributed in England and Wales but the roach alone is found in Scotland up as far as Loch Lomond.

The rudd grows to be a bigger fish than the roach. He is yellow-eyed and his fins are altogether a brighter red. His anal fin grows from a sort of keel while the roach's body is more symmetrical.

Record lists include rudd of three-and-three-quarters to four pounds. The rudd you catch may well be about the size of shoaling perch. The small rudd take with the same eagerness as hungry perch. Cast a worm into a rudd pond in the early morning and the water will often boil with fish. I have caught enough for a day's pike fishing in a matter of ten minutes or so and it often turns out that rudd taken to a pike water containing no rudd prove quite irresistible to predatory fish.

Small fish, however, provide less excitement than specimen fish, those closer to the record list. Ledgering with a good red worm or a lob will take the solitary rudd just as well as it takes the bigger winter roach which are caught in February.

Rudd are often found in midwater when the weather gets colder and will take the bait as it sinks. In summer they feed close to the surface. They will not only take the wet fly – a Butcher or a Zulu – but a dry fly fished on top of the water. They rise freely on a warm summer evening when there is a haze of rain on a south-westerly wind, but if the fly doesn't lure them then a fly and a maggot may do the trick.

Fishing with maggot it is generally better to use two maggots rather than one. The rudd has a bigger mouth than the roach, as well as a bigger head, and he likes a mouthful of maggots, even three, if you like to put so many on the hook.

While rudd may give the coarse fisherman hours of pleasure when he comes across good swims, the trout fisherman looks upon the rudd as a competitor to the trout's world, and this of course is true. Rudd begin life as vegetarians, live on plankton and weed, and move on to take snails, insect larvae and the insects which break the surface to hatch as flies.

In fertile lakes and reservoirs where the stock of food is plentiful, roach and rudd breed up in summer after having spawned among the reeds and weed stems as the natural growth of weed takes place. In a short time waters that supported a reasonable stock of trout become overcrowded with coarse fish.

The amount of food available for trout diminishes and the coarse fish have to be seine-netted or caught up in traps and transported to some other lake or river.

The brassy rudd is hard to kill off. In parts of Europe he and the roach are highly prized commercially. In Britain, however, both are there to be fished for in scores of ponds, lakes, rivers, canals, reservoirs and gravel pits.

Since the dace is one of the fish which, like the rudd, may be sought after as bait, and belongs in the carp family like roach and rudd, it may be as well to include him here. His food, after all, is almost identical to that of the roach and rudd. He too, is often hooked by the trout angler and is generally encountered in shoals.

The tackle used for roach will do well for dace: a No. 12 hook and two or three maggots with the same restrained groundbaiting.

Fish close to or on the bottom in colder weather, and look for the dashing dace on the top of the water in the warmer months.

The favourite flies for trout such as the Pheasant Tail, Greenwell, Wickham and Hare's Bar will do nicely. Use two pound nylon and expect the better ones to weigh about half a pound. Gentle ledgering in the current by lifting the rod and allowing the water to move the bait and lead is a useful tactic.

Ounce for ounce the dace is as good as a lively perch, but you must not expect him in all the waters where you fish for roach and rudd! He is a fish of the river.

There is some danger of thinking you have caught a record dace when you land a chub if you overlook the fact that the slimmer dace also has a smaller head. The scales of the chub are more distinctly to a 'netted' pattern than those of the dace. The dorsal fin of the dace is finer than the chub's. The tail of the dace is forked.

Dace are a fish of southern waters rather than those to the north and west. If a specimen dace should come your way it will weigh around a pound. The record list includes fish from one pound two ounces to fish of one pound four ounces. All the best dace seem to come from East Anglia and Hampshire where rivers are rich in food enjoyed by this lively little silvery fish.

8

Coarse Fish: Bream and Tench

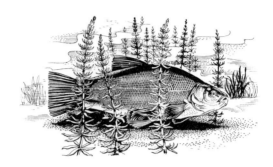

If fish can be compared to animals that live above the water, then bream are like sheep. They feed together. Shoaling in freshwater fish generally takes place at two stages in their development and for recognizable purposes. The first shoaling phase occurs during early growth from fry to fingerling size, and the second when the fish reach maturity and breed.

In the early stage of their life small fish are at the mercy of predators. They haunt the cover in which they were spawned and find food there. They hunt in company and later on venture farther afield. There is safety in numbers.

At spawning time fish associate in groups of male and female, and when the water temperature is right and food plentiful they continue to keep together as the roach do.

But it seems likely that bream stay in company all their lives. Where one bream is caught another will be taken. They come on the feed together. They move from one place to another.

The bream experts sometimes work an area together and close in when one of them finds the shoal. The bottom of almost every lake, mere or river has areas where, through the inflow of water in one place and outflow at another, silt builds up. This happens in rivers where the current is reasonably swift, for all rivers wind or bend somewhere and out of the main flow mud or fine sand will slowly accumulate.

In this rich material the food of fish like the bream is plentiful in warm months, for larvae develop, worms multiply and snails feed on weed that grows in mud.

There are two sorts of bream in Britain, the small silver bream, and the larger and more common bronze bream. The former may run to around one-and-a-half pounds in weight – the record is open to anyone who catches one of two pounds.

The bronze bream may grow to ten pounds. The silver bream has a sort of snub nose. The distance between the end of its nose and its eye is much shorter than in the bronze bream. The bronze bream's eye is less prominent.

There are other features and measurements which make the distinction between bronze and the small silver one more positive, but no one gets very excited about the lesser bream.

The bream specialist is looking for a fish of thirteen pounds. One such was found dying in an East Anglian river in 1971. Later that year, a record bream was caught and weighed two ounces less than the fish found in the water!

Bream are despised by some fishermen, who condemn the species for their

The bream has a deep body and a small head

(Ken Whitehead)

sluggish habits. They are said to be poor fighters because they are winched up out of the mere with little difficulty. The bream of the river is a livelier fish and much more robust, or so say the bream enthusiasts. This, they claim, is because the river makes them so.

In the lake, or places like the Norfolk Broads, bream never cultivate the muscle a fish working against the current must have. The river fish, while they are never quite as big as the average fish caught in still water, may well have become conditioned to a different world and be more active.

Whatever their habitat, bream remain sifters of the mud, stirring up the silt, unearthing the roots of small water plants, sucking in the larvae.

It isn't necessary to use the very fine tackle one uses for the roach, although the movement of the shoal is unseen and the fish keeps out of sight.

Let the angler who fishes for chub or barbel scoff at the bream! Who, at the start of his fishing career, wouldn't like to catch a fish of three or four pounds? A six pound bream isn't by any means out of the question.

When bream feed, and they feed in spasms, they are busy. The problem is to find their feeding place. They are wanderers – there is no doubt of that. So, considering that they are quite big fish and need a fair amount to eat, it is reasonable to assume that when they seem to be off the feed they are sometimes off in another place – feeding! Search for them. There is no better advice.

If you are lucky enough to find a feeding place, make a careful note of its situation and try there again. One of the features of a muddy or silted area of lake or river is the bubbles you may see on the surface of the water, particularly on warm days.

These bubbles are gas from the decomposing vegetation contained in the silt. Often in a bream water it is the activity of the fish stirring the mud that keeps the bubbles breaking up above.

It can't be assumed that wherever you see bubbles on the water there are bream to be caught, but it is a good plan to try all such places.

Remember that most fish forsake the shallows for two reasons – the sun penetrates too well and they are in greater danger from their enemies there. Secondly, the water becomes deficient in oxygen. The fish find it harder to breathe.

Fish the muddy area along the banks in the evening and in the morning. Take a boat and fish in towards the weed beds and places where the bottom is heavy with mud during the day. Shelter is always important to fish when the light is strong and bream may be under cover. Look for them in openings among the weeds.

Since bream, like tench, are largely summer fish and seem to disappear in winter, they may be neglected by the angler in autumn, but the whole business of fishing must be related to the weather.

In a good summer it isn't only the plant life that thrives but insect life and everything depending upon it.

In a warm mild autumn bream are still there to be had and they may be 'gathered' about you as you ground bait from the bank or some old punt moored out on the mere.

Groundbaiting is one of the essentials of bream fishing. Some anglers say that it can never be overdone. The mobility of the bream shoal is such that if groundbait is not enough to hold them they will travel on, just like the grazing animals in the field. So make your groundbait into firm lumps about the size of a golf ball and distribute it liberally along the edge of the weeds or on the flanks of the bed of mud below.

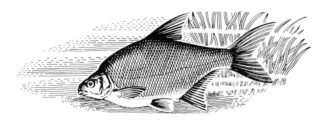

BREAM

Do this, of course, with the minimum of disturbance. Never assume that because the fish can be caught without a fine tackle it is unwary. Too fine tackle for bream is unsuitable on one simple count alone. The fish is a sizeable one. It roots through the mud. It takes your worm or maggots or paste on a hook that must be big enough and strong enough to hold it – Nos. 4 or 6, to six pound nylon on a fixed-spool reel. The rod, too, must be stout but pliable, to give the right action from tip to butt rather than being soft at the tip or throughout its length.

The tackle for fishing where there is a gentle current may be modified a little from that employed in completely still water.

One thing to remember is that where the bream feed the mud may be not only soft but deep. If you ledger with too much lead on the line you may bury your bait. This will give it about as much chance of being found as the little worms or mosquito larvae that hide away in the murk of the bream's activity in the mud.

If, however, you are looking for a really big bream you may use a sliding float and as small a shot as it takes to bring a good big lobworm to the bottom slowly and naturally. This slow descent of the bait often takes the attention of the bigger, bullying fish who dominates the other members of a shoal.

Baits are little less varied than those employed for roach or rudd because the bream really is a bottom feeder. All the different earth worms from the lob to the smallest red will do well. Maggots are greatly favoured and bread or paste in one flavour or another. A ball of paste from the size of a gooseberry to a walnut is attractive to a fish with a large mouth.

Groundbaiting with chopped worms and maggots has one drawback – muddy depressions in rivers and meres are often the haunts of eels. Not many anglers like coping with the tangles the eels make. Eels are meat-eaters and they are not partial to bread and bran paste.

Experience will teach you the characteristic take of different species of fish. The bream does more than angle downwards towards the bait. He stands on his nose to get it. This lifting of the bait and the small shot on the line causes the float to 'uncock'. It falls flat on the surface. The bream gulps in the lobworm or ball of paste and then trundles off like an old man.

Like the tench, the bream is a slimy fish. Handle it with great care for this slime is protective. When it is removed the fish may become prone to disease. It is in any case a species that doesn't live long out of the water. Unlike the pike, it doesn't survive left lying in the wet grass while you attend to something else. Put it back into the water without delay: either into the mere, or if you must collect bream, into your keep net.

When putting a distressed fish back into the river always support it lightly with your hands and have it facing whatever current there may be. Put it into reasonably deep water and never poke or prod it to see if it is ready to go!

The tench is another fish that is the quarry of the idle summer angler, the fisherman who is hooked on the atmosphere of fishing as much as on angling itself.

Tench fishing is for some anglers a picnic, an outing rather like being in a punt drifting along the edge of the willows. Often the occasion becomes framed in memory like the drowsy day on the weeded-up canal where roach were found.

You won't find many tench fishermen pegged out along the side of the pond. The essence of tench fishing is the individualism of the angler who likes his own company – and keeps his secrets.

The tench itself might be labelled a secretive fish. Like the water rail that goes unobtrusively in and out of the rushes, the tench doesn't often advertise its presence. It is there for the observant angler to see when it moves into the margin of the pond, across the mud and on out again.

Tench

(*Ken Whitehead*)

The tench is one of the most beautiful fish found in fresh water. Some tench are a wonderful golden green but apart from being handsome they are also good to eat. They belong to the carp family and have the vigour of the carp.

While you may search for bream in a mere, often the problem with the tench is finding the right pond or lake. Tench have frequently been stocked in farm ponds and pools away from the road. There are secret places carefully hoarded by those in the know, and cherished as the mushroom-gatherer cherishes knowledge of the best paddock.

Someone who knows little about tench may one day tell you that his old grandfather used to catch them in such-and-such a pond, and you will make a discovery that will give you the key to good tench fishing.

The pond or lake may be heavily weeded. In this case you must rake a clearing in which you will subsequently fish. Raking may disturb the fish but it often frees a great many things upon which the tench likes to feed, small animals, larvae and so on. A day after you have made your fishing space you may catch a tench in it.

Remember, when you explore in this way, that fish don't accommodate the angler by feeding immediately he arrives on the scene. The tench could have been there without fancying your bait at the particular time you laid it out. Again, not every angler returns to fish another day where he has had no success, although this is exactly what he should do.

In this kind of searching there is no such thing as free fishing. All fishing belongs to someone, to some landowner or estate. The owner may lease or rent his fishing (whether it is in some pond, lake or gravel pit) to a club or syndicate. He may even issue or sell a number of day-tickets.

If you march over the fields and settle to fish for tench you may be trespassing and poaching at the same time. The golden tench, for instance, is almost certainly a specially stocked fish, and you will bring trouble on your head and have to pay damages if you take out fish that the owner has been at some expense to put in!

The tench is almost exclusively what is called a still water fish. It is rarely found where there is any force of water, although it may be caught where a slow-flowing stream or river joins the lake. It likes the weedbed and the green canopy of the lilypads. Fish over these and along the side of the banks.

The shallows will be more productive in the late evening when the shadows give the fish greater security. If you are fishing close to the bank in shallow water make sure that you have ample cover and that you remain still.

Put the bait (with the very minimum of shot to keep it there – or no shot at all) on to the mud or into the water above the weeds, with the float lying to one side. Make sure the rod is not so drawn back into the brush that it cannot be lifted and used when the tench makes off. Make sure, too, that you have room to handle the rod and the fish once the battle is on.

The tench can be as much as eight or nine pounds in weight, although much smaller specimens of two or three pounds are likely to be your reward.

Fish with a strong but reasonably flexible bottom-fishing rod of split cane, whole cane or fibre glass, a three-piece and around twelve feet in length to give you reach when you have to get over flags and reeds.

It doesn't matter whether your reel is a centre-pin or fixed-spool, but again the fixed-spool is often much easier to cast from when there are obstructions. A breaking strain of three pounds will be adequate.

A fighting tench may be hauled out of the weed with less danger if you use six pounds breaking-strain, but such rough treatment doesn't guarantee the fish being brought to the net and may do permanent damage to a very good rod. Into the bargain you may lose your tackle at the end of it all.

Two ways of taking tench are mainly used, ledger and float. The worm pleases the tench. So, too, does paste. He will take bread, flake or crust, and sometimes the maggot may be the thing.

Judicious groundbaiting where the weed has been raked is advisable. Here you may set up to float-ledger or 'lay-on', using a small drilled or bored shot on the line with a split shot to hold it back a foot from the bait. The float is set on the line so that it is partially cocked when bait and bored shot lie on the bottom. The half-cocking of the float is a useful device. Any movement of the bait causes the float to cock and the fisherman may rest at ease until he sees this happen.

Tench are not what would be called bold in their approach to a bait laid out like this in deep water. They have a tendency to nudge and nibble at the ball of paste and do this for several minutes on end. The float quivers, dips a fraction and steadies again before it finally slides away. A moment before this happens it may all at once go flat on the surface, but then the tench is off for the cover of the weed bed. He bores deep and the advantage of the float-ledger tackle is that it is light. There isn't a heavy dangling weight to catch up in weeds or tree débris littering the bottom.

When you are fishing in very muddy ponds or meres it is best to use no weight at all. Let the well-moulded ball of paste carry the hook to the mud. Use a No. 8 hook for paste and a No. 10 if your choice is for bread crust or maggot. The bigger the fish, the bigger the hook. The big tench has a leathery mouth. If the hook is small then it must be needle sharp. The first rush is the one that puts strain on the tackle, the one when the poor quality hook or the slip-shod knots you have used may find you out.

If you want good tench fishing, get up very early. In midsummer the best of tench fishing may be over by eight or nine in the morning, so you must rise before the lark or, alternatively, go fishing in the evening.

Like the bream, tench often reveal their presence when bubbles rise. Unlike the bream, however, they will surface and splash along the edge of the weeds, particularly in the morning.

There is no danger of confusing your tench with other fish. He is broad-tailed, thick-bodied. His fins are always dark although his colouring ranges from light olive to golden green. He has a small barbel on each side of his mouth.

The best fish to date have always come from lakes, ponds and gravel pits, mostly those in southern counties, parts of the Midlands and East Anglia. Record lists take note of good specimens at about seven pounds. One of a few ounces over nine pounds would, at the moment, put you out in front.

9

Coarse Fish: Carp, Chub and Barbel

Everyone who fishes for carp must begin somewhere, but of all the fresh-water species the carp is probably the one to which it is best to come with a little experience. If you are already making progress in catching roach and bream, for instance, then you know about bottom-feeders and the way to handle them. But the carp is warier than other fish. Shy isn't the right word for him.

In addition to feeding on the bottom like roach, bream and other fish, he takes food on the surface, particularly at night. There are times when he wallows in the shallows or cruises about like a whale nosing round the estuary.

There are several sorts of carp including the little crucian carp which many fishermen say is hardly worth bothering with. The carp that really tops the list is the wild one which, as Richard Walker proved away back in 1953, can grow to forty-four pounds. The capture of this monster carp made history for carp-catchers. Why hadn't such a fish been caught before?

The carp, a common food fish of a large part of the continent of Europe, thanks to the spread of the Roman Empire, came finally to Britain in the Middle Ages. It had been fished for or netted out long before there were fishing seasons but no one, it seemed, weighed their fish! This, of course, must be nonsense. Good fish when they are not authenticated with exact weight and the names of witnesses, tend to grow larger with the passing of time! Pike legends support this. Why then were no big carp caught with rod and line?

The methods available in the old days were restricted by the sort of rods, reels and other items of tackle used. No one had gone after carp with single-minded determination to catch the biggest of them. Better reels, more suitable rods and a careful study on the part of anglers of the Richard Walker school resulted in the first of the really big carp being caught.

Many years have passed without that fish being bettered, but some fine carp have been caught since. More people are fishing for them than ever before. Somewhere, some day, Richard Walker's carp will be surpassed. Mr Walker himself believes this.

What approach must you make to carp fishing? It isn't easy to find a carp specialist who will take time off to instruct you in the art of carp fishing. You must rely upon the books. You must become as efficient as you possibly can at the business of coarse fishing and study to be skilled as well as observant in everything about fishing.

Never be half-hearted. Always do things with thoroughness in putting your tackle together, in preparing to fish, in laying out the line and keeping as much out of sight of the fish as you can possibly manage.

Small carp may be caught much more easily than big ones. The crucian is one of these. Catching this chubby little carp, which may run to about one pound, and now and again one and a half pounds, will perhaps teach you that the carp is very much a sucking fish.

You will use a rod such as you might take for roach or bream and employ light float tackle. Most of the baits that you use for the bream or roach will do for this little carp which is found where it was established, along the Thames valley and the south-eastern counties of England.

Perhaps it was never considered worthwhile transporting the crucian beyond this area, and those responsible for its introduction were only interested in its novelty. Use cloudbait and brandling worms, maggots, bread or paste. A No. 12 hook is about the right size.

You will often find the crucian carp close to the bank of those ponds and gravel pits passed over by the angler who is only interested in really big fish. When you catch this small carp you will find that he lacks the barbels at each corner of his mouth which mirror and common carp have.

Immediately you graduate from everyday fishing for roach, rudd, bream and small carp, you will have to consider much more sophisticated tackle. Not every item the man who fishes for big carp considers important is really essential to catch carp. Remember the expert isn't after just any carp. He looks for specimen fish at least, and sets out to catch the big one. So he has all kinds of things such as illuminated floats and bite-detectors as well as what might be included in a survival kit – sleeping bag, iron rations, and footwarmers, perhaps!

The bite-detector lets the carp fisherman have his forty winks. His sleeping bag lets him stay with the thing to the bitter end. He fishes not just for two or three hours, but a day and a night if need be.

The expert's rod will be at least ten feet in length. It will be a two piece more often than not. It will have a positive action throughout its length but be sensitive enough to cast a comparatively light bait.

The fixed-spool reel is by far the best because it allows line to travel out with-

Record carp of 44 lbs taken at Redmire Pool in September, 1952, by Richard Walker.
The fish is displayed by Peter Thomas

(*Richard Walker*)

out danger of the very sensitive carp being checked as he moves away. Fishing where the handling of rod and setting up of tackle is easiest often means that you will forego the chances of hooking a giant.

We must walk before we can run and the carp expert himself probably fished in a lot of ponds before he tried the difficult swims. A fibreglass rod without metal ferrules is the most robust and most durable rod for the job. One that weighs about eight to nine ounces may be used with line of about eight pounds breaking strain.

Hooks from No. 2 to No. 8 will certainly cover your needs, and a good big landing net that isn't too heavy to handle. If you are fishing completely at ease and need a simple indicator, remembering that sometimes your float may be out of sight, a piece of silver paper loosely rolled round the line will serve. As the bait is moved and the line tightens it will finally slip through the silver paper as this meets the first ring.

An electric bite-indicator would be perfect, but a beginner does well to make haste slowly. He is better keeping an eye on everything and cultivating his patience. A casual approach will never make you a good fisherman!

There are a great many different ways of catching big carp. Bait may be suspended above the fish or be allowed to float up from the bottom. Occasionally a crust of bread may actually be used as a float for the bait down below. Bait suspended may be laid out over supporting weeds, or, where carp come in close to the bank, may float in the water directly beneath the rod point.

Always cast bait gently. The carp is not just a wary fish but a well-camouflaged one, dark on the back, greeny brown to greeny-black, and a perfect blend with his surroundings. Never assume that he isn't there and you are going to have a long wait. The certain way of making it a vigil is to disregard the fact that care should be taken when a bait is put out.

While bread is very popular, there are many other baits that may be tried.

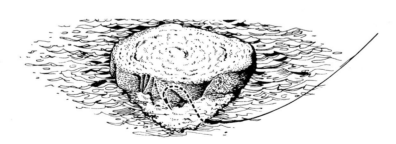

BREAD BAIT

For the moment consider the way a crust float may be rigged. Thread the hook and a foot or so of line through the floated crust and immediately underneath the crust pinch on a small lead shot to keep it in position. The hook is then baited with a piece of flake bread, the point being entered in the flake side and secured in the crust side of this bait. Sometimes the line may be threaded through the 'float' crust more than once. The flake bait should not be very big but adequate to cover a No. 6 or No. 8 hook. A larger crust may be put on where a sliding weight is used on the line and the hook allowed to rise with the buoyant bait so that the offering appears on the surface.

Carp feed on floating débris of this kind, but remember that many water birds, some of them much bolder creatures than the fish, also like to gobble up floating crust. Playing a swan might seem an exciting novelty but it is a distressing thing for the angler and may easily prove fatal to the swan – if he doesn't break your rod. Again, this is a sound argument for keeping your eyes open at all times.

With a reasonable degree of watercraft, surface and margin-fishing is possible by day. At night there is a problem in handling a fish that runs through obstacles not easily made out by the angler on the bank but it cannot be denied that surface fishing is the most productive at night.

You may, as most carp fishermen do, lay out a rod for both methods of fishing. The conventional ledger is not greatly favoured by the expert. He likes

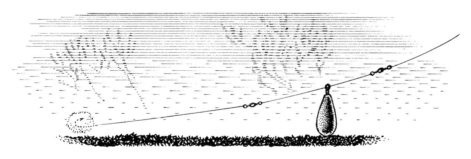

RUNNING LEDGER

to use no weight at all, feeling that the carp reacts to the drag of the weight before the hook can be set. If ledgering, use a minimum of weight and a swivel as a stop. The rod point can be angled down towards the water or even submerged in it. This allows line to run out freely. When the line begins to slide off the spool you will take up the rod, engage the bale arm and strike from the reel, having made sure that the frictional drag on the spool was sufficient for this to be done positively before you begin to fish.

Small potatoes (one expert uses tinned potatoes only) are boiled and the line put through them with a baiting needle or a large darning needle. The potato needs to be quite soft and have its skin peeled away. Occasionally flat sections of potato will be used where there is a danger of the small round potato falling through the carpet of weed.

The other everyday baits for roach, barbel and chub may also serve. although it is wise to remember that the carp is no everyday fish. Offer him what he is known to like best, and experiment if the popular bait fails.

The chub is a very different fish from the carp, although he may be as wary on occasions. He is not a still water species. He lives where the pickings are good.

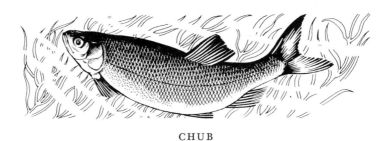

CHUB

He takes shelter under the willows and rises to insects. He may sometimes be said to be a pest to the trout angler fishing in the shady corners and hoping for something good from the hole below the tree.

The chub is not a fish for the table and he receives the full-time attention of only a few anglers. It may not be hard to catch small chub in the eddies of some trout stream. It may be possible to feed them a little groundbait and catch them in the sun-dappled slow waterway between the sallows and willows. They take the maggot, paste and moulded cheese. They are a handsome fish and don't give up as easily as the sluggish bream.

The bigger chub, however, behaves with the shyness of the roach or the estuary mullet and feeds in the evening when the light fades after ten o'clock. You must wait for the evening chub to feed and you may need a bite indicator as you would for the carp).

There is an old and well-tried device that cheese-fishing chub enthusiasts use. Having moulded your small knob of cheese to the size of a hazel nut and cast your hook with whatever bait you have decided upon (which may not be cheese but a maggot, for instance), take this small piece of cheese and mould it on to your line where it stretches between the first and second rings of your rod. This will make the line droop a little. Since the cheese is only put on the line

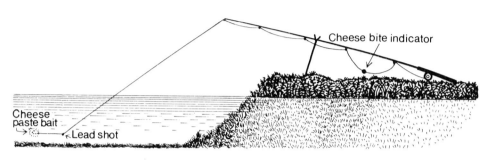

BITE INDICATOR

when it has been cast, any lifting of the bait by the fish will let the ball of cheese drop and you will have warning of the take. If the chub runs the line will tighten, the small knob of cheese will break loose but with no damage done as the signal for battle is given.

The fixed-spool reel is best. With a low breaking strain line you can cast neatly into places where chub shelter.

Your rod doesn't need to be a heavy one and its length will depend upon the width of rivers or streams you will be fishing. There are occasions, however, when a fine line will result in nothing but frustration. Big chub moor themselves in channels between the weeds. They take fiercely if they can be approached without disturbance – free-lining (without weight of any kind) is one of the best ways of doing this – and they must then be held, even hauled back from the jungle.

Since they weigh between three and four pounds and can be a pound or so larger (the record stands at seven-pounds eight ounces with many fish of greater weight left in dispute for one reason or another), fishing for big ones you will need a stout rod.

The bigger chub are not shoal fish but solitary in their habit, like most other fish of great size. Small or large, when chub feed they are voracious and they will take almost anything that is offered from bread to sausage meat. They have

Chub being landed

(*Ken Whitehead*)

a sweet tooth and can be educated into taking fruit of different sorts simply by feeding the swim with it. Biscuit crumb is another bait that may be gently fed into the water above the place where the chub locates himself.

Immediate groundbaiting works better with chub than other freshwater fish. In exposed water where it runs shallow, the rolling ledger offering worm, maggot-paste, or cheese is a good method.

Lift the rod until you feel the lead bumping, allow the bait to be carried a short distance and settle down to give the chub a chance to take it. Repeat the 'roll' after a while and remember that your hope is that the chub will work up to your bait.

A large worm is probably more easily detected than most other baits, with the exception of the minnow. Chub are predatory and feed on small fishes like minnows and gudgeon and so you may turn to baiting with minnow as you

Barbel grow to a good size in southern rivers

(*Ken Whitehead*)

would for big perch, trout or pike. You may, of course, find you have ceased to fish for chub, and all your knocks will be from perch or eels!

To catch barbel you will have to go to much livelier water. This is a fish that is a sort of cross between the carp, who has barbels on his mouth and feeds on the bottom for a good part of the time, and fish that need a great deal of oxygen, being unable to survive where the water is dirty.

The barbel hugs the gravel and seeks his food by touch and taste there. The fast current slips over his stream-lined body and even presses him more firmly down in a place where a fish like the carp couldn't hold his own for a minute.

Only now and again does the barbel come to the top and show himself as he jumps. This may be because the oxygen has been drawn from the water during the day. Sea trout and brown trout also jump out on warm evenings.

Groundbaiting is absolutely essential with barbel. They must be fed and it is wise to bait before the day and accustom the fish to finding food in a particular swim. The barbel is strong. It needs to be, to stay in the weir pools of the Thames and the fast waters of some of the other rivers in which it does well.

A river weir is often good barbel water

(*Ken Whitehead*)

Even a small one of two pounds will fight to stay out of your reach and will use the current to put a strain on your tackle.

Ledgering is the method if a float may not be watched or kept under control. Lobworms, bunches of maggots and good-sized knobs of firmly moulded paste are the baits. There are, however, many places where fishing from the bank isn't a good idea. The place the barbel chooses may be far out of reach of the angler either on the edge of the weir or below it, and then a boat or a punt must be anchored in order to fish.

BARBEL

This kind of fishing has a certain danger about it. Keeping a boat anchored close to a weir calls for vigilance and boatmanship. It is all too easy to let pre-occupation with snagged tackle or the use of a net overcome natural caution while the water flows over the gunwale. Disaster may come at a frightening pace.

Use hooks from No. 4 to 8 and line of about six pounds breaking strain. A really stout rod will cast the ledger weight you find necessary in a particular current, and stay the rush of a very powerful fish.

Your fish may well be only three or four pounds, but could run to double figures if you are lucky. The best barbel on record were taken from the Hampshire Avon, the Dorset Stour and the Thames. It is not found in Ireland or Scotland, but it is caught in a number of other rivers in Yorkshire and the Midlands.

Some of the fish now excluded from the records were caught out of the coarse-fishing season by salmon fishermen using worms, or were foul-hooked when a weighted spinner was allowed to trip across the bottom of a weir pool. Among these were three around sixteen pounds in weight.

10

Game Fishing: The Technique of Casting

The species of fish known as game fish are those that spawn in the colder months of the year; trout that breed in October and the winter months which follow, salmon and sea trout that follow the same pattern but are migratory. All three of these may be caught with spinner or bait. Indeed most of the larger trout are taken with bait and many of the big salmon are caught with a spinner.

The basic technique of spinning for pike or perch is varied a little with game fish. But it is when the angler comes to fly-fishing that the whole business is complicated by special rods and lines. Some trout fishermen apply themselves to worm fishing. There are many game fishermen who never touch a flyrod, but the technique of fly-fishing is refined.

Fly-fishing invariably appeals to those who have imagination and who strive to acquire skill at anything they take up. The newcomer may be baffled by the number of rods he finds in the tackle shop and the great variety of fly lines, for the rods will vary in length from around eight-and-a-half to twelve feet or more and weigh from about four ounces to more than half a pound. The lines will range from level ones to forward taper with many variations in taper and weight for different conditions of water or use in rivers or reservoirs.

Casting for the novice is a matter of timing and practice but initially it is to put a suitable line on a rod for wet fly-fishing. (I will write about wet fly-fishing later.) At its simplest it involves casting a straight line, dropping the fly in a place from which it may be worked over the fish and kept in positive control of the line at all times.

For the purpose of explaining the technique of casting, all that is needed is a fly of some sort tied at the end of a nylon cast of three yards length used with a nine foot rod. The lines will be as heavy as the rod will carry and probably a tapered one. A heavy line can be managed in the early stages with much greater effect than a light one.

The fly at the end of the cast should be a fairly heavy one, too. When it comes to practical fishing the large fly and the heavy line will be used on a bigger rod, perhaps for sea trout or salmon.

Casting a fly is something like an old-time coachman using his whip very gently, so gently, that the animal would be unaware of its settling!

A flyrod is not a whip, however. It is resilient like a whip but it has a degree of 'backbone' to enable it to push line out and to carry it in the air, back, and then forward again, straight and true and falling on the water a fraction of a second after the fly itself alights.

The rod is held in the angler's hand with his thumb gripping it on top of the cork handle and in line with the rod. The action of casting is never from the

ORTHODOX GRIP FOR FLY CASTING

wrist but always from the elbow. The force imparted to the line is applied when the rod has been lifted (and the line with it) and the rod has reached a point indicated by the hands of the clock at eleven. The backward movement is made to a point indicated on the clock face at one, and never beyond this point!

A count of one-two-three may serve to control the backward movement. The forward movement begins after a brief pause to allow the line to straighten out behind and the forward movement is halted at eleven o'clock, on the same one-two-three count.

In practice, the line is being lifted into the air, halted by the rod, allowed to roll back over the angler's head again, until it straightens out in front of him and comes down on the water.

This explanation undoubtedly leaves out a lot about precise timing and the force to be exerted in rolling the line back and driving it forward once again. A simple count of one-two-three will do nothing to prevent the line falling in coils about the angler's shoulders or lashing down on the water immediately in front of him.

Some people who explain the technique compare the forward and backward force with that employed to throw a small knob of clay or mud by fixing it on the end of a short stick and aiming it at some kind of target. This forward 'flick' is achieved by bringing the movement to an abrupt halt. When such a movement is made with a flyrod the tendency will be for the line to crack like a whip. Almost invariably this whipcrack means that the cast has snapped and it, and the fly or flies, sail away in the wind.

It is possible to damage a rod by too enthusiastic casting but an hour or two's practice with enough line out to make the rod work should be enough to enable the amateur to grasp the principles. Too little line is as hard to cope with as too much.

From a nine foot rod lay out about twice that length of line. Do it away from the river on a well-trimmed lawn where there are no trees or overhead wires to cause frustration. Lay the rod on the ground and the line too, straightening it to its full extent. Go back and pick up the rod. Switch the line into the air above you, doing so once or twice until you have the feel of the rod and line.

Almost everything you attempt to do will come to nothing at this stage. Look at the fly and see what is happening to it. If necessary put a small piece of white paper on the hook so that you can see it more readily. Keep your elbow firmly in at your side as you lift the rod.

The action is never limp and pliable but positive, a positive backward movement, a positive stop, a pause and a positive forward drive to bring the line up over and again.

Remember, never backwards beyond one o'clock, never forward beyond eleven o'clock before the stop is applied. Immediately the strong forward action has been halted the rod may gently follow through, coming down to something like ninety degrees with the body as the line finally settles on the water.

It is important to master the technique of casting first. There are many frustrations in fly-fishing arising from poor technique. The greatest disappointment is simply that of failing to catch any fish. Fish are simply scared away by bad casting, the rod flapping in the air, the line falling with a great splash on the water, the fly dropping in like a ship's anchor!

There are schools of casting. It generally pays to get lessons either from a qualified instructor or some good fisherman kind enough to spare you some of his time. More can be achieved in five minutes with a rod in the hand than in reading thousands of words that try to explain the force applied in carrying the line back and driving it back over the water again.

Poor casting may be improved but basic mistakes often remain with an angler all his life. There is much more to casting a fly line than simply putting the line straight out onto the water! It may have to be swept in under an overhanging tree, thrown upstream against a gusting wind, laid other than straight, but in a question mark so that the flow of the river will carry the fly over a certain run where the line must then straighten.

There are many different sorts of cast, roll-casting, backhand casting, left-handed casting. In the first instance a lake or a reservoir may seem the place to practise once the basic principles have been grasped. Undoubtedly wide open water will be attractive, but a river flows, and in the early days the fly-fisher-

WET FLY FISHED DOWNSTREAM

man may find that some of his less well contrived efforts are improved by the current! The line is carried and he is able to recover the loop or the bungled cast in time to fish.

Remember that the whole purpose of the exercise is to place a fly or a lure in the window through which the trout watches the surface. The trout doesn't care how the line was cast. He really shouldn't know such a thing happened. He certainly won't take your fly if he is frightened or made suspicious.

Once the line is down it travels on the current, or you must make it travel to impart movement to the fly. The fly may move of its own accord, hurried by the current, washed through an eddy. The trout that takes this moving fly may turn with it in its mouth and the hook will go home but he may feel the steel of the hook and eject it from his mouth long before you are aware he has taken it.

The purpose of the straight cast and direct control of the line all the way to the fly is to make sure that the fish can't reject the fly and is hooked almost as soon as he tugs at it.

In wet fly-fishing the fly will be beneath the surface, an inch or so perhaps, but certainly out of your sight. Your guide to its position in the water will be the line in the surface. If the line is anything but straight you can be sure that the cast, too, is swinging and slack and this will often mean that the whole thing becomes futile. The fish is pricked and goes down to keep away from something of which it is now suspicious.

The most disappointing failure for the fisherman is the fish he almost lured, the one that followed the fly, took it for an instant and rejected it at once!

The importance of learning how to cast a straight line cannot be over-emphasized. When skill in this department has been achieved you cannot fail to succeed as a fly-fisherman.

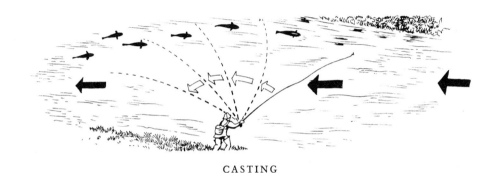

CASTING

Casting a dry fly is not quite the same thing. A straight line is important in dry fly-fishing. If a fish rises on the surface of the lake or pool the fly-fisherman must contrive to cast to the rise without delay. His line must fall as lightly as thistledown. His fly must kiss the water and rest within a foot of the ring where the fish rose. The fish that breaks the surface invariably hooks himself as he turns down, despite all the pretentious nonsense some angling writers have to put out about 'striking the fish'.

If the line falls in loops the fish that takes the fly from the surface may well eject it from his mouth again and so a good straight line can hardly be bettered, but by the nature of the take, the straight line is not vital in dry flyfishing. There are times when the floating fly and the line may be allowed to drift, or when a good length of line will be cast so that the fly may be allowed to move slowly down over a rising fish.

On the whole, casting a long line, certainly a line much longer than that needed to reach the fish, produces problems. It is hard to control a fish, even when it hooks itself quite firmly, if it makes a run or dives into the cover of rocks or trees shading the water, carrying more line than the angler can immediately recover.

This comes down to technique applied to the water being fished. To begin with, knowing that fish are only close to the bank where submerged rocks provide shelter, put out enough line to reach the feeding area or likely places for trout to be sheltering. At first, fish with the shortest manageable length of line. When this arc has been searched with as many casts as are necessary to do it thoroughly (sometimes one may do), draw off a couple of yards more line and repeat the process.

Do this again until you have fished out the water within reach, after which you may move farther along the bank, going as far as need be to enable you to do the same thing all over again.

On the river you will always contrive to move upstream, for fish lie heading into the current and when they take in this position they are more surely hooked than when the fly is taken and they lie downstream of the fisherman.

In the lake, and sometimes in the river, you may step in and wade, but remember wading too brings its own problems. Disturb the water and you drive away fish; step out from your background of bank cover and the fish may see you much sooner and you will have gained nothing. While you are wading and casting you may overlook the bushes which formerly gave you cover and now constitute a casting hazard should they entangle your fly. Many a good fly rod has been badly strained when this has happened!

Assuming that you have acquired a degree of competence with the flyrod you chose to learn the technique, you will soon discover the limitation of the elementary equipment. A short rod for a small stream, a sweet pliable rod for fishing the wet fly on the stream or small river, a rod with a stiffer action to enable you to put the dry fly on the target – these are things which will either induce you to change at once to specialized rods and lines or force you to modify your technique to allow one rod and one line to do for all kinds of fly-fishing.

A rod of nine feet will let you fish for brown trout in most rivers and will serve on a lake. It won't be quite the thing for a sea trout which could weigh eight or nine pounds and maybe more. It won't do for the salmon and it will take punishment when you try to make it do on a choppy reservoir where the fish are deep down and big at that. The line too, will sometimes need to sink to reach the big trout or the salmon in the pool. It will not only have to suit the conditions and the fish but the rod. It is useless fishing a light line on a heavy rod and very foolish to fish a heavy line on a delicate flyrod.

In these matters, having discovered the shortcomings of general purpose tackle, you will do well to consult the specialist anglers fishing the reservoir,

A rainbow trout in fine condition

(*Ken Whitehead*)

plying the big salmon rod, fishing for sea trout after dark or going quietly up the stream to fish the dry fly on some clear run among the weed banks.

In no other branch of fishing is there such a selection of rods, reels and lines as in game fishing because of the different sorts of water on which fly-fishing may be done. Two-handed salmon rods are commonly used on quite small rivers. On larger ones they are the only suitable thing. On very big rivers very long rods, some around eighteen feet in length are still used.

What is called Spey casting is delightful to watch, even if it isn't a technique for the beginner, and requires an incredibly thick line to carry the fly over a salmon as much as forty yards from the place where the angler is wading.

Both tapered line and a tapered cast give the angler such advantage in putting the fly over the fish without disturbance that every fly-fisherman soon comes to them. It remains a matter of choice whether the line is a straightforward tapering one or one of the other sorts of line such as a 'long belly' or a reverse tapered line which have certain advantages in ease of casting. Tapering a cast may be done to a formula – so many inches of two pounds/four pounds breaking strain and so on – because a cast must go out as smoothly and fall as straight as the line itself.

Tackle dealers can supply tapered casts but they are expensive. On the other hand casts can be made up by the fisherman himself after he has bought spools of nylon and studied the knots needed in cast-making and illustrated on page 33.

It is a wise plan to keep the number of knotted lengths to a maximum of three and not to become obsessed with the need to taper the cast to the extreme. It is also wise to settle to fish a tapered line and practise to achieve skill with the particular combination of rod, line and cast. Flitting from one thing to another often teaches little. Nowhere is it more apparent that the angler must make haste slowly than in fly-fishing.

Among the most important considerations is the cost of equipment. A good fibreglass fly rod will cost perhaps £20, although at the moment some may be had for less. A good rod will last a lifetime. A good wet fly line should last for years. It too, will cost a fair amount of money, something between £6 and £8 at the moment. When a good reel will cost as much as the line and often a little more the beginner will do well to proceed with caution. He will discover what he needs, what suits his hand, and finally, what he likes best, no matter what the other fellow uses.

11

Game Fishing: The Brown Trout

Although salmon fishermen would never agree, the highest degree of art in fly-fishing is in fishing for brown trout. Trout fishing differs from salmon fishing in that the trout belongs where he is found. He lives in the river, stream or lake for all of his life. He survives because he knows his environment, whereas the salmon is only a visitor, a migrant who may be caught in the estuary, on his way up the river, or in the feeder stream where he goes to spawn.

When a trout lives in a pool beneath a willow tree, or breaks the surface at the lower end of a weedbed every warm summer's day, he presents a problem to the angler who would catch him. He is feeding on things the river produces at a particular time. He knows what his food looks like as well as you know your favourite dinner. He knows not only the shape, size and colour of his food but the way it moves. Only when he is ravenously hungry can he be lured into taking something impulsively.

It is much more necessary to fool the fish when fly-fishing than when fishing with bait. When it comes to the very small items of a trout's daily diet the secret lies in imitating those insects and fishing the imitation in such a way that it looks very like the living thing.

Of course, it is impossible to make an insect that looks remotely like a living one, for no imitation quite matches the delicacy of the wings of gnat or mosquito. Nothing can be exactly the shape and size of a tiny beetle that flicks its way across the fine gravel or swims across the surface of the water where the trout finds him.

The trout 'fly' is often a shade bigger than the natural insect and invariably lacking in fine detail. It is a lure, when all is said and done, the smallest lure that anyone fishes on the end of a line. Think of a creature as big as yourself using a delicate rod, a tapering line with a fine nylon cast coming down at the very end, to a tiny, gossamer-winged gnat. This small thing must be made to sail out on the breeze, drop gently into the ruffled water of the stream where the weeds are swept back by the current, and there be inspected by a fish who knows what a gnat should look like!

The brown trout lives on a number of things found on the bottom. The fly-fisherman's choice lies among these insects, beetles, larvae, water snails, freshwater shrimps, worms, grubs and so on. Small trout live where they can, rarely in deep water where the food is plentiful, and more often than not in fast current where they must be alert and ready to dash out to take anything that comes their way.

This is the nature of the brown trout's existence in the early stages of its life. The small fish crowd one another. The bigger fish battle for the best feeding situations and have their stations in the pools or behind boulders. Here the supply of food is good, perhaps because of the inflow of a feeder stream, or a river entering the lake.

Swift mountain trout stream

(Ken Whitehead)

The largest of the brown trout will eat lesser fish as well as flies and other insects. He will never move quite so readily to snatch down a morsel as his smaller relatives will. Here, then, is the fly-fisherman's world if he goes in search of brown trout, fast water or slow eddies, shallow water where small fish are to be found by day and into which the big fish only move at dusk. The fly must reach the fish but there is no guarantee that when it passes over them they will show interest.

Brown trout hardly ever move to order. They have their feeding times and times when they will hardly look at anything. The early months of the fishing season find the brown trout out of condition and eager to feed. By May and June the fish have recovered and later become less eager. By later summer they have hardly any appetite at all except on cool days.

The mystery of fly-fishing is not just where to fish, but when and how to overcome one of the most weather-sensitive species that swims in water.

The wet 'fly', as you have been told, is fished beneath the surface of the water where no winged insect lives. A natural fly that dies and falls onto the water remains floating and doesn't sink. In the sense that a winged artificial 'fly' represents a living insect, only one designed to float on the surface is really a fishing 'fly'. The sinking 'fly' is something else. Being an imitation of the insect before it hatches or emerges from the underwater world, it can only be a nymph, a grub or a beetle. It is often only a very general representation of one or two of these and not much more than a rough lure.

The brown trout, however, doesn't know what the intention of the angler is. The fish swims in the water and takes what appeals. When it is frightened by the angler it takes nothing!

Flies for brown trout vary a great deal. Everyone has his own particular favourites, but a great part of fly-fishing is to have faith in the flies being used. When the angler believes in himself and the flies he is using, success follows. When he doesn't, his lack of confidence causes the whole thing to fall down.

To begin with, leaving the selection of flies for the moment, let us assume that you are fishing wet and will use a cast with two droppers, that is, three flies in all. Most wet fly-fishermen insist upon three flies although the beginner may find he has fewer tangles if he sets out to learn with no more than two. The action of the wet flies has to appear natural to the feeding fish. This means that they must either be kept moving by the fisherman or be moved by the undulation of the water lifting and lowering the line and cast so that the flies move accordingly.

The fisherman doesn't often rely upon this natural movement but makes the flies travel in short, sink-and-draw movements. The trout itself rarely lies still in the water waiting for such things to happen but, like a raven riding the air currents, rises and goes down, moves from side to side, advances and retreats a

Fly-fishing for trout in a chalk stream

(Ken Whitehead)

little. He does this to maintain his place in the river perhaps, but more to keep a good lookout.

When the flies come into view he may rush at them or make a slow, shark-like inspection before he takes. The take is a short and sometimes not very distinct tug. Sometimes the fish turns away and is well hooked. But sometimes, and often on warmer days, he will take half-heartedly.

No wet fly-fisherman relies on the trout hooking himself, but in response to the tug tightens the line by lifting the rod. Almost immediately a trout of any size responds to the hook by swaying and rushing away. Sometimes he will bore down and sometimes rise out of the water and crash back down upon it again in an effort to break free.

Let the line run without letting it become slack. Keep contact with the fish and be prepared either to recover line if he comes back towards you, or give him a little if he has the strength to overcome the weight of your finger on the reel.

Never allow the playing of the fish to take too long, or in fact last a moment longer than is necessary to bring him in over the net. Over-concern in playing the fish involves a risk of the hook working loose as it enlarges its entry point.

Now that the trout is over the net, raise the net and lift him clear of the water. Never, never remove the hook while the net is still above water but carry your

LANDING NET

fish clear of the bank and there deal with him. Inspect your cast and the flies on it before resuming fishing. Often a barb may be broken off in the process of playing or landing the fish. The fisherman who hurries things to catch another may find he has gained nothing and lost a great deal!

The matter of what flies to use is one upon which few old hands quite agree and novices will debate until they are old. There are many hundreds of patterns. A dictionary of trout flies may be had. There are as many volumes on patterns of flies as there are cookery books. The truth is that most of the flies recommended are good or will be good on particular occasions. It is also true that four or five general purpose wet flies will serve an angler in most situations. A boxful of different patterns makes choice more difficult and success often less certain.

Having said this, I must recommend half a dozen patterns any one of which may be disputed by an expert living in another district. To deal with imitations of the natural insect (some masquerade under the names of the men who invented them) first on the general list is a fly called Greenwell's Glory. Canon Greenwell was an ardent fly-fisherman. He gave his name to a fly that was closely related to the dun, which hatches on streams, rivers and lakes for a good part of the fishing season.

There are several duns. The lake olive, for instance, is a larger fly than the dun most encountered on the stream. Canon Greenwell's version in different hook sizes (10, 12, 14) covers them all, although it must be said that the worthy churchman's recipe has been varied since he first used it. A Greenwell to cover the nymphs of the dun, and a Welsh pattern of fly to cover the beetles, a Coch-y-Bonddu, which should be fished from one of the droppers of the cast.

To complete a cast of three, the Black Gnat, which serves as an imitation of a number of dark nymphs.

As an alternative to this set of three, imitating the duns again, the Mallard and Claret. Another old favourite, the March Brown, probably the best-known of all fishing flies and another very useful fly, or Wickham's Fancy, with the third on the cast perhaps a Partridge and Orange.

Six flies will never do! If six are not enough there is no end, but we may look at more when we consider the flashers which are purely lures. Then we have dry flies which may correspond more closely to the winged insect that alights to deposit its eggs in the water, or hatched out after rising as a nymph from the bottom.

Flashing flies or lures are even more numerous than general representations of the natural insect. All the imagination and ingenuity of the fisherman has gone into the making of this kind of fly. The ingredients call for everything from the fur from a hare's ear or a hedgehog's belly to a wren's feather.

In the main, of course, the lure has tinsel, flat silver, oval silver, round silver, gold, green or blue tinsel and feathers dyed bright red or blue. Among the flashers the choice could be boiled down to two or three, the Peter Ross, the Butcher, the Jersey Herd (made from a bright Jersey milk bottle top). The Peter Ross has a rouch of red to represent the gills of a tiny fish and its 'wings', which slick back on a silver body, are teal feathers that look like the scales on the sides of the fish.

Use of such flasher flies as these must be with a lively action. Small fry never hang in the water close to a large hungry fish. Flies like the Butcher and the Peter Ross are best when kept darting along near the surface.

The dry fly is something quite different. It needs to be set down delicately. It must sail on the water with maximum buoyancy. It is rarely successful as a surface fly if the hook sinks and hangs below water like an anchor. Its use requires close observation of the natural insect and its behaviour as it takes off or settles. The fly must be a much closer approximation in size to the living insect than a wet fly needs to be.

The dry fly can be fished in three ways, but the conventional and 'purist' way of fishing the dry fly is simply casting to the rising fish. This, moreover, is the most exciting way of fishing a fly.

The other two ways are to cast the dry fly at random, leaving it on the surface to drift in the hope that it will attract the attention of a hungry fish, or drawing the fly in after it has been cast, causing it to make a wake on the water. Fishing the ripple in this way is rather like wet fly-fishing, except that the fly is buoyant and disturbs the surface of the water continually.

The choice of a dry fly is more or less settled by the fish. There are some patterns of dry fly which represent no particular or precise species of dun or sedge. Most rough sedges (the fly which emerges when the caddis grub has passed through the nymphal stage) are general representations of a great number of flies which no one has yet listed.

You cannot fail to recognize the sedge. It is heavy in flight compared with the graceful olive dun. It is a ponderous fly with heavy wings and equally heavy legs. The lake trout love it when it is hatching in large numbers.

SILVER SEDGE   MEDIUM SEDGE

TROUT FLIES

The olives and the stone flies, the more delicate flies of both stream and lake, need more careful attention. They may be observed with the aid of binoculars. The angler who identifies the insect and can cast a fly to a feeding fish will always do much better than the one who says that 'near enough is good enough'.

If you can't name the fly it doesn't really matter. What is important is that you should be armed with dry flies respresenting such insects as the olive duns, the iron blue dun, the spent fly (known as the spinner), the pale watery duns where these hatch and perhaps the Yellow Sally.

The choice must be made to suit the water and the locality. It is futile, for instance, to fish the big mayfly on a northern river or stream where the mayfly doesn't breed!

The dry fly, if it is well-constructed, floats with little help except perhaps a little oil or a previously applied silicone spray. It will of course sink if it becomes water-logged. But it is dried by false casting and re-oiled or even greased on occasion. Its attraction depends upon its ability to stand high, to dimple the surface without breaking it, and to give an impression of something light and delicate to fish turning in slow circles to inspect it.

Since dry fly-fishing calls for the use of only one fly, and the technique often

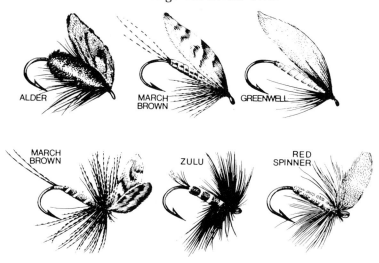

ALDER   MARCH BROWN   GREENWELL

MARCH BROWN   ZULU   RED SPINNER

TROUT FLIES

allows stealthy correction of a bad cast, many young anglers will find that they can catch fish more easily fishing in this way. But this will not apply on those very clear chalk streams. Here the 'educated' brown trout has seen it all before. He will give the most skilled handler of the most perfect dry fly only one chance. Few beginners will be faced with the problems of the angler on the expensive chalk stream!

The beginner must not become too involved in debate about exact imitation, which is really something for the expert fly-tyer. He needs to observe what fish are taking and find an approximation to this insect in his selection of dry flies.

What the surface-feeding fish sees will be argued until the end of time. One most important thing concerned with what it sees or doesn't see lies in the fact that dry fly-fishing generally calls for brighter sky. It is never very successful on a totally overcast day. There must not be a glaring sun, but ideally sunlight and cloud. The water must not seem warmer than the air. Fish don't feed well when this is the case. Flies must be seen to be hatching. Fish need to be seen to be feeding.

Sometimes a dry fly offered on a dull day when fish don't appear to be looking for food will produce an unexpected boil, but only rarely. Dry fly-fishing isn't a haphazard business. It shouldn't be the last resort. Like any other kind of fishing it must be done with confidence and skill.

To make a fish rise, swirl and take the fly – once you have achieved this there will be no other sort of fishing that can grip your enthusiasm and imagination quite so much.

12

Game Fishing: Sea Trout and Salmon

While brown trout fishing depends upon the study of a fish and its behaviour in a place from which it moves only a short distance, the pursuit of migratory fish calls for a different study and different tactics. The runs and 'lies' of the salmon and sea trout must be known, for without knowing where the salmon lies the angler fishes blindly.

There is another thing. At different times rivers are high or low. This means that the runs diminish in depth, and some of the lies become so shallow that fish are not found in them. The salmon has some way of measuring water level, or tasting the degree of pollution as it increases in times of drought, and keeps out of parts of the river where the low level might lead to danger.

When a salmon has been a long time in the river its colour changes from bright silver to something like pillarbox red. It is what is called a stale fish. It has little interest in anything that passes through the pool and ignores a worm bait, a prawn, shrimp or a spinner.

Only when the freshet comes – the cleansing flood that results from perhaps two days of rain – will the red salmon move on. When the water is clear and high these moving fish plough on up to the very source of the river. This, after all, has been their objective from the moment they passed out of the salt or brackish water of the estuary.

Salmon anglers are excited by the sight of fish showing first at the tail of a large pool and then at its head. Often as a fish leaves at the top of the pool another will show at the bottom. This indicates a procession of fish on the move upstream and what anglers call 'the run'.

After a few days this eager upstream rush may slow down. The lately invigorated salmon will rest a while in some big pool below a weir or a bridge.

Here the expert salmon fisherman will ply his fly or cast his spinner, knowing from experience exactly where the fish is moored.

Now a salmon resting in a pool must keep himself alive where he is. The current is often a powerful force. The fish, of course, rests in whatever depression or sheltered place he may find on the river bed, but from time to time he may rise and examine something passing over his head, move forward a few yards as though about to forge on, and perhaps drop back to a place well below his original position. Sooner or later he will lie within a yard or two of the same spot.

The experienced salmon fisherman doesn't even have to see the fish doing this. He knows his ways. He knows, above all, the watermarks, the river marking stones or touching the roots of trees. Observation enables him to cast the fly or the spinner in the right place when the river is high or again when the level has fallen.

River lore, then, is essential in salmon fishing.

When an angler is lucky enough to have explained to him the secrets of where the salmon lie, he is up against one or two other almost equally puzzling things. Salmon don't take the fly or lure to order. They rarely take a fly after dusk, for instance, as the sea trout does. They have taking times that vary a little according to the month.

In bright light on unshaded pools one may have to wait until the angle of the sun is low. Salmon are keen-sighted although they are less wary than an old brown trout. Sea trout are even more highly sensitive to light and shade, and very sensitive to any disturbance of the water when the river's level has fallen.

For the beginner it pays first to concentrate on one fish or the other and to consider the three ways of catching salmon or sea trout – by the use of the fly, by spinning or by fishing bait.

On almost every river there is great competition for the most productive places. On every river there will be one or two pools from which most of the salmon caught by rod and line are taken. If it is a river where both salmon and sea trout run, and there are quite a few where the sea trout are not found, there will also be pools coveted by the eager sea trout fisherman who fishes in the dusk or in the dark.

We will suppose that you want to fish for sea trout with a fly rod. The flies need be only a size larger than the everyday wet flies you use for brown trout. Although you may use three on a cast, considering the bushy nature of the riverbank and the fact that there are trees in the vicinity of most of the best sea trout runs, you may be better equipped with only one.

In fly-fishing for sea trout, as well as salmon, much of what is done and what happens is 'blind'. The angler doesn't see his fish. He really doesn't want to because when he can see the fish the fish can see him. This is one of the reasons

Seatrout river

(*Ken Whitehead*)

why so many sea trout fishermen go to the river at twilight. They can then have the dark background of the bank and fish a short line without danger of a very wary fish detecting their presence on the pool.

There are as many kinds of sea trout fly as there are wet flies for brown trout but to simplify everything we will use a very successful fly, the Teal, silver and blue.

Casting a fly for sea trout requires a good straight line, cast a little upstream and kept as straight as possible by finger control of the line as it moves down and across the water without wake or sign of drag. The fly must not be dragged or jerked or made to move unnaturally as it sails in an arc which the angler follows, whether he can see his line or not, allowing the rod to steer the line down the run without strain.

Most takes happen when the fly is somewhere between directly in front of the angler as he looks across to the opposite bank, and halfway between this and a point directly downstream, that is, at an angle of forty-five degrees. Sometimes, however, an eager fish will follow the fly when it is retrieved straight upstream at the end of a cast.

The fresh run sea trout is a tender-mouthed fish. Its flesh is often so soft that tightening the line may pull the hook from its jaw. On the other hand, it is also a most virile fish and not one to be hauled out of the water without a battle. A net big enough to take a twenty-pounder should always be used even if the average sea trout caught may be no more than a pound. Even a nine pound fish will give a great account of itself and needs to be handled with care.

Once again, never attempt to remove the hook from the fish's mouth or take him out of the net until you are well away up on the bank. When you hook your first sea trout you will understand how easily you might have lost it had you fished a cast of three flies and one of those flies snagged in a sunken branch.

The disturbance caused by an encounter with a good fresh-run sea trout of any size may convince the novice that he should go elsewhere to try his luck, but often patience is rewarded. A second and then a third fish may come struggling through the shallows below the pool and turn at the fly sailing down across his path.

The period during which sea trout take is often short-lived. All the way down the river fish will move quite unpredictably and be heard rolling, or splashing their way through pools and runs below overhanging bushes, and then the thing will be over. You may fish on until the grey mist before dawn and catch nothing more.

If you would try your hand with spinner or bait you may fish not only in the evening but throughout the day, as indeed, you may do with the fly. The chances of catching fish will undoubtedly improve although you may not always catch sea trout but sometimes a salmon, sometimes a brown trout or grayling and often, if you are dangling a worm, an unwanted eel of two or even three pounds weight.

In deep pools you may choose a sinking line. At night, using the same wet fly, you may find that a sinking line is not only hard to locate but difficult to lift out when you want to cast again, and it makes a loud report as it breaks from the water. Casting a fly for salmon is, by comparison with the most refined dry fly-fishing for brown trout, no more than lure fishing. The secret lies in knowing the size of the fly to use. Patterns vary and the choice is great, although you might be advised by someone who knows the sort of fly the salmon on your particular river go for most readily.

The technique of casting is the same as for sea trout, upstream and across, allowing the fly to sail naturally as the current takes it down and keeping the line straight. Let the fly 'swim' until it is straight downstream and then bring it back with a sink-and-draw movement if a fish hasn't shown interest in the meantime.

Fish are sometimes prompted to take the fly at the very end of the whole business when the fly is being recovered. A take before this may seem to indicate that the fly has lodged in some sunken tree or rock. The fish may even hold still for several minutes before moving upstream or turning away but you will know the lively feeling of a sinuous fish well-hooked.

All that remains is to play him, giving him line when he must have it, applying strain when he runs towards trees or bushes half submerged or tries to leave the pool for some rocky gully leading to one lower down. There are some people who count the minutes and talk about a minute per pound of fish. This is generally nonsense. A fish that bores into heavy water and strong current tires quickly. A fish that can dance his way from one deep to another without meeting a strong current will take a lot of time unless the angler is prepared to have his cast broken or his rod tip damaged. A stale fish gives up more readily than a fresh run one. There is no measure of time against weight.

Salmon fishing with a spoon is not very different in technique from fishing with a fly. The spinner will be cast slightly upstream, the line brought under control and the spoon or spinner allowed to move with the current, across and down in an arc. The current itself will impart action to the spoon or make the spinner spin and only very rarely will the angler need to impart any movement to the lure by the gentlest turning of the reel handle. What the salmon sees is a silvery sprat or some other small fry, fighting its way to the shelter of the bank perhaps, but being forced back by the current.

If this small fish has any power to stimulate the salmon's recollection of what he bolted down so eagerly when he was feeding in the sea, he turns and snaps at it. He feels the hook. He lunges and perhaps rises to the surface and swirls about the pool for a minute or two. He bores into the current. The angler, if he can move, tries to get downstream of his fish, keeping in mind the fact that if the fish gets below him the river will help it escape. If the salmon can be kept upstream the force of the current will tire him.

Salmon are more often gaffed than netted or tailed. They are sometimes 'beached', that is, hauled onto the shingle and dealt with there with the priest.

Gaffing calls for skill. Catching a salmon is a heart-stopping excitement. Playing and bringing one to the bank may leave an angler exhausted and shaking if he has never had the experience before. To fail at the last minute because the gaff was misused is mortifying.

Having played the salmon until it is tired out and lies on its side, bring it within distance of the gaff, very carefully change the rod from right hand to left if you have not already done so, and aim to drive the gaff home firmly and accurately somewhere as close to the head as possible, if you can. This will leave the better part of the fish undamaged although you may fail and ruin the famous 'middle cut'.

Once the gaff is in, keep a firm hold on it and the rod and step back, up out of the water, and onto the bank. The gaffed fish is a piece of muscle from one end to the other. It could never jump the falls unless it was strong and resilient. It may recover and break free at a critical moment when you are just above the water, so give it as little chance to do so as you can. Take it well back and make an end of it as quickly and as painlessly as you can.

Worm fishing for salmon or sea trout is the least exciting way of taking them, and using the shrimp is not a whit better. Shrimping or prawning is generally frowned upon by dedicated salmon fishermen but the fact remains that the majority of salmon caught on our rivers are taken by bait fishermen using worm or prawn.

Both require sound knowledge of the lie. Indeed, shrimping or prawning (the tackling up will be explained elsewhere) is almost a matter of bumping the bait against the salmon's nose until he snaps at it.

The shrimp or prawn needs to be weighted, of course, as the bunch of worms needs to be ledgered, and held in the current so that the salmon, waiting for some change in the water, may have more than enough time to inspect it. The take may be indicated by a brief tightening of the line and a slight bellying of the nylon as the worms or prawn are mouthed.

Thereafter the salmon will either move away or drop back to where he was before he took the bait. In the latter case the angler discovers he has had a fish on the line when he thinks to see if his worms or prawn have gone.

The fish is generally well hooked, but rarely obliges by letting himself be docked like a liner. On the contrary, he will forge upstream and find the roots of a tree round which he may entangle the line, spilling from the fixed spool reel or ticking off the multiplier before it is noticed.

Rods for fly-fishing for salmon and sea trout are more robust and generally heavier than those used even for lake or loch fishing for big brown trout. They are mostly from ten-and-a-half to twelve-and-a-half feet in length for moderate rivers, although they may be longer for the larger rivers of the north. Again the choice of material is likely to be fibreglass nowadays, although the best salmon flyrods are split cane.

The rod that will manage a sea trout will serve for a salmon in most cases, but the two-handed, heavy salmon flyrod is the choice of the man who specializes and confines himself to the king of fish.

THUNDER & LIGHTNING   JOCK SCOTT   BLACK DOCTOR

SALMON FLIES

Filling a flybox with salmon flies is a rich man's indulgence. Salmon flies are like women's hats, highly decorative and expensively trimmed so that a beginner, unless he is rich, will confine himself to the fly for the river in two or three sizes recommended by the old hands, adding to these as he gains experience.

The use of different lines for different conditions of water is a pitfall into which the novice can easily drop. This may be avoided by a careful study of the old hand who rarely carries a great amount of tackle and knows that as good a fish is taken on a well-presented fly as on the most highly-refined equipment the salesmen can sell. For fly-fishing, a solid rod that isn't too heavy and isn't so sensitive that it calls for a prolonged battle with a fish; for spinning, a well-made spinning rod (of about ten feet) that will cast a small spinner of one or two inches in length.

Fly reels for salmon should have a wide drum to take enough line, and be of solid construction. A more refined fly reel can be used to balance the rod chosen for sea trouting.

When game fishing for sea trout, one almost always has to wade and needs to use either thigh boots or waders. In the latter case brogues are the best footwear. They may be felt-soled or nailed. Thigh boots with rubber soles are dangerous in some places. So, too, are felt soles under certain conditions. Nails give no hold at all on smooth rock and perhaps the best thing for safety is a wading staff which may be attached to the belt by a thong.

13

Sea Fishing: Mackerel, Bass and Whiting

Fishing in the sea was, until thirty years ago, something rather like paying a penny for a lucky dip. The fisherman hardly knew what he might come up with, and generally didn't really care so long as it was an edible fish or something very big. The tackle was crude. Only a few people paid much attention to the great variety of baits available for different kinds of fish.

It was well known that mackerel could be caught on almost anything from a 'last' of fish to a bit of silver tinsel. Whiting committed suicide so long as there was the merest fragment of lugworm on the hook. This is still true.

On certain occasions when they are feeding ravenously, mackerel can be caught on a line with no more than a shirt button as a bait. They can be caught four or five at a time, as anyone who has gone out with the old fisherman to troll for them knows. But it is refinement in tackle that makes the catching of any seafish exciting.

To go to the extreme, any sort of fish could be brought up from the bottom with explosives. No one would want to be party to such wanton slaughter and it certainly wouldn't be fishing.

The way to fish, intelligently and for enjoyment, is to refine the method, to give the fish an equal chance and to employ skill to overcome it in its natural element.

A mackerel on a light rod will give as good an account of itself as any fresh-water fish. It is a streamlined creature, built for speed. It is not only fast but greedy. It takes the spinner and rips away with it. A great many mackerel have always been caught by deep trolling from a boat, handline fishing, but we are really concerned with fishing with rod and line. As many mackerel are taken from the shore or the jetty as are caught with rod and line from a boat.

There are two or three well-tried ways of catching mackerel. Each of them depends upon the presence of the shoal. Very rarely will you catch a single mackerel. Where one is, the shoal is. Where one feeds, the shoal is feeding. They travel together. They get hungry and feed together, but one at a time is good fishing.

While the commonest method is undoubtedly the use of the spinner, mackerel are also taken on feathers. From a boat this may be done with rod and line to good effect simply by using a bomb-type lead at the end of a cast of six or eight feather 'flies' consisting of dyed cock hackles whipped to a hook. The flies are cast or lowered into the water and worked by raising or lowering the rod at regular intervals. It is the movement that lures the fish. Sometimes more than one mackerel will seize the flies.

The advantage of feather fishing from a boat is that the angler who finds nothing happening in one likely place may move to another. Mackerel move predictably with the tide but they don't always come in as far on every occasion, nor will they always come in at the same place.

The reason is quite simple. Shoreline currents carry plankton. All kinds of marine life depend upon plankton, including fry and whitebait upon which fish like mackerel feed. Where the jellyfish sails along, there is plankton. Where the plankton is there will be fry upon which shoaling mackerel love to feed. This applies, of course, to other surface-feeding predatory fish such as bass. Where fry and sand-eels swim, the bass will forage.

It is surprising how large a spoon the hungry mackerel will take but as a general rule something less than the very biggest kind of spinner will serve best for the mackerel. If a small spinner such as a Mepps is used it often pays to put a torpedo or barrel lead on the trace about eighteen inches ahead of the spinner. This serves two purposes. It enables the small spinner to be cast as far as possible to cover the available water and it keeps it down at the right level while it is being retrieved.

Mackerel will rise and turn to a spinner in a mad rush and sometimes pursue it for a considerable distance, one or more snapping at it and imparting a slight tug to the line.

It sometimes pays to slow the retrieve down a little, but it never does to let the spinner cease revolving. The mackerel will turn away in disdain once they have discovered the nature of the lure. This doesn't mean that the fish won't take the lure when it is cast once more and kept at an even speed, but there is always the danger that the spinner was only on the fringe of a moving shoal and while the fisherman was experimenting the shoal had time to move on.

Since mackerel move near to the surface when they are not actually chasing food on the surface and through shallows, the use of the last – a small tapering slip of fish cut from the underbelly and slipped over the barb of a hook – is another device that brings results.

The last is, of course, not really a bait but a lure. It is taken for whitebait fry or a sprat. There is one advantage to it which is that when fish are caught a fresh supply of lasts is available.

Mackerel are not discriminating. They will take almost anything that is shaped and moves like a fish – a milk bottle top, for instance, or a small bit of tin.

There are a number of legends about mackerel and their scavenging habits. In some places no one will eat them because they are said to eat the flesh of drowned sailors. In some parts of Ireland you will be told that the mackerel are wary and almost impossible to catch when the first shoals come in, but later on, when they have been feeding in shallow water for several weeks, the bright sun blinds them and they can be caught without trouble.

There can hardly be a greater contrast in the angler's approach to mackerel than the way he sets about catching bass, and for a good reason. The bass, until he grows big, may shoal like the mackerel, but he is a much more nervous fish and every bit as fast. The shoal bass move in company with the incoming tide, scouting the crannies in the rocks below the beard of seaweed in which prawns and other small animals shelter.

Bass move on into the brackish water of the estuary in the same way and at the same time as the even more shy mullet. They move out again, perhaps an hour or an hour and a half after high tide. They can never be caught in shallow water where the angler must stand without cover.

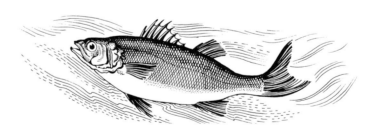

BASS

Bass fight like salmon and indeed old seaside landladies are said to have coloured their flesh with cochineal, dying them pink to persuade visitors they were sitting down to fresh caught salmon.

Bass are taken both by spinning and by the use of bait. Spinning isn't productive until there are jellyfish about and shoals of fry have been seen on the shore, or sand-eels marked by hungry gulls feeding beyond the estuary.

The Toby spinner, a large Abu spoon that dives and sways as it is recovered, must be heavy enough to stay down and not be dragged until it skitters along the surface of the water.

A most useful alternative to the spoon is the imitation sand-eel of which there are several patterns, some more lifelike and successful than others.

The bass fisherman knows that on a rocky shore he must fish in rough water. Bass are so keen-sighted that they are in and away before you can blink twice. They steer a course well clear of anyone perched on a rock above a calm inlet.

Bass are a robust, salmon-like fish and when they grow big they forsake the company of others and travel along like the old-time policeman on his beat.

On occasions they will swim steadily after a spinner with their mouths open without taking it, but when they are really taking they will give a good tug and rush off into the deeper water and have to be persuaded back again with care and skill. Here, as in salmon fishing, the angler needs either a net or a gaff. The bass fights all the way and it is often much harder to get the gaff into him than it is to do the same thing with a salmon. A net, on the other hand, may be dipped into the water and the fish brought over it. A good bass will weigh six pounds although the records cover fish of much larger size.

Since bass seem to take to surface feeding as the gulf stream warmth penetrates northward, it was at one time thought that it was useless to fish for them outside the summer months. Now although bass forsake the colder surface areas in late autumn, they are to be caught on the bottom like many other species of fish.

Ragworm is one of the best baits for bass. Even if there is no guarantee that the fish that takes the bait will be a bass, it may be ledgered or fished just off the bottom with a small balsawood 'float' attached to the line six or eight inches from the baited hook and about as far from the weight. This lifting of the bait brings it more readily to the attention of the fish searching for food. In slack water floating the bait in this way keeps it out of reach of crabs which may be scuttling about looking for something to eat.

As with most forms of bottom fishing in the sea, where a variety of different sorts of fish are present there is always a problem in trying to catch a particular species. Discriminating between bass and conger is simple enough. The conger lurks in rocky caverns and a very rocky bottom is not the best one for bass fishing. On the other hand there will be very little weed on a sandy bottom, and few boulders to shelter the kinds of food the bass likes, so a study of the seabed at low water is advisable. Equally important is a knowledge of good fishing marks. This information can be acquired by watching other fishermen and learning from their example.

Pictured with this 72 lb conger eel, the best from Dungeness
for many years, is enthusiast Ron Grigg from Edenbridge, Kent
(*South East Angling and Photographic Services*)

Bass have certain channels along which they feed. The exact location of such
feeding grounds needs to be carried in one's head. A few yards to the right or
left of a feeding ground may be quite barren and unproductive, but consider

the fact, for instance, that bass are fond of ragworm. In the sort of ground in which ragworm are dug you will find the sort of fish that like ragworm. It follows that you will avoid soft, silty areas, except in summer, and confine your fishing to those places with a reasonably hard, gritty bottom in which boulders are numerous. Bass move through such areas as the tide turns, an hour or so before high tide and the same period afterwards.

Fish on the bottom rather than in midwater. Keep in contact with the weight and be ready for the bass to lift it. Give him time to swallow the ragworm and, when bottom fishing, make sure that your line is strong enough to hold a fish that just might top fourteen pounds!

The rod and reel? For shore fishing, a good solid fibreglass beachcaster and a sound multiplier well-filled with line – as much as it will take, bearing in mind that you may have a fish that will run out with the current off the headland or perhaps hook a skate that will have to be persuaded to give up a suction grip on the bottom well beyond the leverage of your big rod.

The hooks for bass? Sizes 4, 6 or 8, but remember that the bass is always wary of the hook and the larger sizes are less successful.

As an alternative to ragworm you may use squid, a piece of herring or mackerel. The latter have a strong oily 'taste', particularly when they are a little high.

Bait should be cast out just beyond the breaking surf, the area where stones and grit are being churned up revealing crustaceans and other marine animals to fish that feed with the tide.

In summer sand-eels and freshly-caught prawns may be used and either allowed to 'swim' freely on the tide in places where bass regularly show, or fished with a small and inconspicuous float used more as an indicator than a support for the baited hook. Sand-eels always attract feeding bass. One solitary sand-eel seeming to have been injured will be taken on the tide even when eels are not shoaling along the estuary.

While there are many devoted and specialist bass fishermen, whiting and other fish such as codling and pollack rarely have all the attention of the sea fisherman. The reason is quite simple. All of these sorts of fish are plentiful in season. None is very hard to catch. The whiting takes a fragment of lug-worm and doesn't need to be offered ragworm, which is much harder to dig. It isn't a discriminating fish. Where the crabs don't steal the bait the whiting can be relied upon to find it, except perhaps when there is an east wind or some acute change in weather.

Whiting fishing is really paternostering and rigging the tackle to keep the bait out of the way of crabs. Ledgering is equally suitable on the right bottom, but here one may fish with more enthusiasm for flats, flounder, dabs, plaice or even skate.

The whiting, say the old sea anglers, is the cat's fish. It is best cooked in milk. It doesn't make an appetizing meal fried or grilled, which a plaice does. It is watery and almost tasteless if it is cooked too newly caught.

A big one might be classed as one of three pounds or more. The records include fish up to six pounds. The average whiting popped into the strawbass and taken home for the cat is usually about half to three quarters of a pound: one worth filleting and cooking, about two pounds.

Next to the whiting in the novice sea-fisherman's list may be the codling, a ravenous little barbelled fish known to have been caught on a codling's eye or a piece of gill membrane.

Codling, like whiting, have their season. They often crowd the river's course in an estuary in the colder months of the year. It hardly matters what bait is used. Anything will do from lugworm to limpet or mussel. The pollack, which is not even as much of a cook's fish as the despised whiting, is a fish that doesn't give up without a struggle, whatever his size, and he, unlike the whiting or the codling, turns readily to the spinner and rises to the fly.

Pollack prefer the rocky shore. An outsized pollack might weigh as much as twenty pounds although these monsters are taken in deeper water in the vicinity of old wrecks and underwater obstructions. The shoreline pollack is more likely to be a small one of two or three pounds.

The baits for pollack are ragworm, fished as for bass on the tide, prawn, sand-eel, or a last of mackerel used in the way a cast of feathers might be worked in the current. The eager pollack takes almost any kind of spinner or lure from the Mepps to the imitation sand-eel. Once he is hooked he dives for the cover of the rocks. He must be pumped up or he will soon begin to fray the line on barnacles, as the mackerel does when hooked near rocky ledges. Boat fishing for pollack in bays leading to estuaries is a pleasant occupation on a sunny day.

In some districts another bottom feeder with a slight resemblance to the pollack may be encountered. This is the pouting. There is not much justification for confusing the two, however. The pollack's outline is angular. His dorsal and anal fins all give the impression that they have been cut from cardboard with a pair of scissors.

The pouting's head is rounder. His lower jaw is barbed. His dorsal fin is high and shark-like and his body laterally compressed. He is often called the beginner's fish, perhaps because it is hard to avoid catching him. He feeds on worms, sand-eels, shrimps and other marine animals.

Unlike the gallant pollack, the pouting puts up little fight. He takes almost any bait that can be rigged on paternoster tackle and is never a very big fish.

It should be said that while fishing for the common sea fish the angler will sooner or later hook something he would really rather not catch, the weever, greater or lesser. The greater weever is more frequently encountered fishing from a boat, but the lesser weever, which grows to perhaps half his size, has the same poisonous spines and should always be pinned down and destroyed with a knife.

The weever's spines inflict worse pain than the sting of a jellyfish and no one should put his hand to this brightly coloured ugly little fish. To do so may be to risk being hurried off to hospital or at least having first aid for swollen and very, very painful fingers or hands.

14

Sea Fishing: Sharks Great and Small

Who doesn't want to catch a big fish? One of the really big fish in the sea is the shark. He may be outweighed by the whale, but he is a ferocious fish and he can be caught on rod and line, as everyone knows.

Around British shores, sharks are not a danger to swimmers. But they do come within reach of the would-be shark fisherman with the good fortune to own a boat or the means to charter one. It is also possible to book up with a boat owner who takes parties out after those species of shark generally encountered in our not-so-warm seas.

Four kinds of shark are fished for from boats – porbeagles, makos, blues and threshers. The last is an extraordinary fish because, not being armed with the frightful teeth of the man-eater, it has been provided with a scythe-like tail. It uses this tail to strike birds and injured or sickly fish which it may encounter on the surface of the sea.

The thresher can grow to as much as one thousand pounds in weight but such large ones are never encountered in the north-eastern Atlantic and those areas around Cornwall and southern Ireland most favoured by shark fishermen. The British record takes account of threshers between one hundred and fifty and two hundred and eighty pounds.

The larger sharks are makos and porbeagles. The blue shark comes at the bottom of the list with record-worthy specimens between one hundred and fifty and two hundred pounds. Makos are listed between four and five hundred pounds, porbeagles from two hundred and fifty and four hundred pounds.

Sharks in British waters are invariably migrants moving here to breed, although the monster basking shark (it doesn't respond to a lure and isn't caught on rod and line, being a shark that lives on plankton) is thought to breed in the depths of the Atlantic and only travels round our coasts to enjoy vast quantities of plankton.

All four sharks might be taken on tackle used by a conger fisherman, but the tackle of the expert in pursuit of the record will be an outside multiplier (a big-game reel) on a big-game rod with locking ferrules and harness fittings. The outfit may cost hundreds of pounds but it is possible to hire such equipment and the boat owner will generally see that everything needed is on board before he takes his clients out.

The question of where to fish for the shark is one that can't be answered by fishing marks. These marks are areas in which bottom-feeding fish congregate because the supply of food is plentiful. Shark are predators and follow shoals, so the shark boat is steered by a man experienced in the ways of fish. It may be a matter of luck and what is called the rubby-dubby, a bag of offal lowered over the side to attract hungry fish. Where the shoals are the shark follows.

SHARK

The technique is to bait with a small fish, mackerel or pilchard, offered in a similar way to the pike fisherman using dead bait, although there is no need for two floats. The float employed for the shark will be about the size of a fully-grown turnip. A shark turns over as he takes the bait and runs when he feels the drag. The battle is on once the angler had used the powerful rod to drive the hook home.

A long, wide-gaped gaff is driven into the shark's tail once he is played out. The tail end of the fish is lifted clear of the water so that a noose can be slipped over the tail. This is an essential precaution. The jaw of the shark is very hard. Should the hook drop out the shark (and the gaff) may plunge into the deep.

In the shark fishing ports of Cornwall, tackle dealers hire out rods, reels and other items of tackle against a deposit, and will almost certainly recommend a reliable charter boat.

A less exotic sort of shark fishing is the pursuit of the tope, which can often be caught from the beach as well as from a boat. The tope, however, isn't anywhere near the big game class of sharks although the skate almost qualifies, both as a monster and a member of the shark family.

Like all sharks, the tope is tenacious and a really voracious fish. He, too, is a traveller. He isn't found in the same place continually. There is no such thing as a tope 'mark'.

The tope goes where the shoals are, and again the place to fish is a matter of instinct on the part of the experienced fisherman. There are, of course, certain waters and certain channels along which feeding tope move in summer. The tope fisherman knows these places. He also knows the nervous, hesitant way the tope noses around his herring or mackerel bait before he picks it up. This is the way of predatory fish when they come upon an item of food that doesn't dart away. Like a scavenging dog they sniff at it and examine it for a minute or two before deciding that it is something good to eat. Then, having made up their minds, they take!

Tope fishermen will tell you of battles tope have given them on occasions when their reel bearings became hot and threatened to seize, or their rods bowed to the water and the end rings went under. The tope doesn't know what it is to surrender without a fight. And what a handsome fish he is when you see him, blue and shining in the sun-drenched sea! Alas, this beauty fades soon after he is pulled into the boat. Since the tope is not among the really edible species of fish the angler would do well to put him back before he drowns in air!

You need a long trace to fish for tope. They have an extraordinary ability to wind the line around their tails and can quite easily break or fray nylon, so the trace must be long enough to ensure this can't happen. Six feet of stainless steel wire or woven cable will be adequate. The line will be about thirty pounds breaking strain. The hook size should be 5/0 and attached to the trace by means of a swivel to overcome the tope's gyrating tactics, which are designed first to tangle and then break even a woven trace.

Bait should be freshly caught, but a frozen herring, although it may be difficult to keep on the hook when it is thawed and soft, will serve at a pinch. The bait is drifted behind the boat, weighted by a sliding lead with a swivel stop ahead of the trace. Tope mouth the bait before taking it.

It is sometimes necessary to float the offering above the seabed to avoid the clutches of hungry crabs.

When fishing in channels along which tope pass, you may encounter the less spectacular dogfish. The 'dog' has the tope's habit of switching his tail and turning his body to lock himself to the trace. But he hasn't the tope's 'get-up-and-go'. He doesn't fight so much as writhe and squirm. He comes up like a struggling eel rather than a true member of the shark family.

The dogfish isn't everyone's favourite catch whether it be the spotted dog, the smooth hound or the spurdog. They are all despised fish because they hunt in packs and do great damage to nets once they become entangled in them. Dogfish is edible but no one seems to think very highly of it, no matter how it is served up.

Perhaps the only man who welcomed dogfish was the old-time painter and decorator who used the rough skin of the dogfish to rub down old paintwork. A dogfish's skin is said not to clog up as sandpaper does. It is certainly very rough and abrasive which is one of the reasons this long, slimy, ugly fish is able to fray an angler's line if he hasn't used a wire trace.

Most dogfish are caught by accident rather than design when an angler sets up to fish for conger off the rocks, or moors himself to fish in towards the shore. The frustrating thing about catching dogfish is that in places where the pack hunts other fish depart and the angler who begins to catch dogs might as well do likewise.

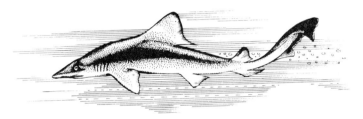

DOGFISH

Not many sea anglers who find themselves with a skate on the end of their line think of themselves as shark fishermen. There is nothing very shark-like about the skate, whether it be the common grey, the sting ray or the thornback.

Rays and skate are equally predatory on other species of fish but as they are incapable of snatching them with their mouths they adopt another technique. 'Flying' like some night fishing heron that beats across the pond, the skate keeps a lookout for its prey, a crab, a lobster or some fish busy rooting among the marine plants on the edge of a clearing. When it sees what it is after it simply alights, covering the victim with its great 'wings' so that there is no possibility of escape. The skate doesn't lack the ability to chew up the fish or crab it has caught once it comes down upon it.

There is nothing under the sea more like a large bird in the air than a skate moving from one feeding ground to another. Small fish seek the shelter of the forest of weed. One caught in the open has nowhere to go. The skate falls upon it.

Both the grey skate and the thornback are common catches of the inshore trawler that harvests the flat fish of the bay. The thornback is a smaller fish than

SKATE

the grey skate which, in some British waters, grows very big indeed. Thornbacks are more often taken fishing in gravelly areas between rocks.

The sting ray is a summer visitor which the beach angler catches now and again, and finds himself pondering how to remove the 'sting' in the tail.

If you really want the big skate then you must go out in a boat and fish where the big skate are found – places off the northern Scottish coast, south of the Shetlands, around the Isle of Man and the coasts of Ireland. The records include one or two monsters above two hundred pounds in weight but these, of course, fell to the expert using techniques designed to capture big fish of this particular species.

The grey skate that goes over the hundred pound mark pleases anyone lucky enough to bring it up. Thornbacks of twenty pounds are big enough for most shore anglers to haul through the tidal currents.

One aspect of the skate's behaviour when it has bolted the bait disconcerts the beginner a little. The fish settles down on the bottom and its wings become a great suction-pad. It must be prised loose before it can be brought up. Only a sound reel and a stout rod will cope with the strain.

As soon as the skate has relinquished his hold he applies one or two other tactics that require some counteracting. His wings once again come into operation. He turns them up and immediately becomes a great water-filled vessel hanging on the end of the angler's line. Everyone knows how hard it is to pull a bucket out of deep water!

The skate makes it as difficult as he can. Perhaps he tilts a little. The angler relaxes pressure on the line. This is a fatal thing to do. Now the skate lets whatever current there is carry him like an upside-down kite as he heads for the bottom once again. If he finds a new hold the angler has everything to do again.

If the skate is a really big one this will be a trial of strength not only against the fish but the undertow.

Once the skate is on the surface he must be gaffed. Unless he is something for the record book and the photographer from the local newspaper the best thing to do with him is to cut him up. Only the wings of this cartilagenous fish are used in the kitchen. The rest should be tipped over the side. A taste of blood always attracts predators and scavengers.

While skate may be taken on a number of baits the best baits are small, freshly-caught fish: a small mackerel, for instance, which the skate 'collects' as he cruises over the feeding ground or watches as it comes slowly tumbling down after you have cast.

The skate isn't always on the move. Part of his time he lies in wait, shuffled down into the sand in the manner of other flatfish. His eyes look upwards. He breathes through spiracles or breathing holes placed just behind the eyes for he can't breathe through a mouth buried in the sand. Now the skate is almost invisible and a perfect blend with his background.

The tackle best suited to the capture of the skate is the ledger although many sea anglers using a paternoster have hooked and landed a good thornback. Catching a skate on paternoster tackle comes about by the paternoster drifting and the bait lying on the bottom.

Ledgering is the best method because it allows the bait to lie where the fish can come upon it. He has time to mouth and then swallow it without being aware that the whole thing is attached to a weight at the end of your wire trace.

The trace should be three or four feet in length. The line needs to be around fifty pounds breaking strain. As with tope, and the more respectable members of the shark family, a gaff is also needed. The rod should be short and stout if used from a boat, but long enough to carry the tackle out to the feeding place if fishing from rocks or beach. The reel, as in all angling for large fish that put a strain on angler and tackle, needs to be a smooth-running, well-made one, preferably with a three to one or four to one recovery ratio.

If you go out to where the big ones are you will discover that nothing happens to order. You will have to wait for the skate. This isn't because skate are not hungry fish. The bigger they are, the more food they need to keep going, but they in turn have to wait. Fish and creatures such as crabs and lobsters upon which the skate preys move when the tide turns and very little may happen at slack water. It depends on the run of tide and the underwater currents, points which the experienced off-shore fisherman knows all about.

The mark is generally found by lining up places on the coast, one perhaps to the north-east, another to the east and yet another to the south-east. This is arrived at by sailing so far in one direction and sighting a second point a known distance away.

Here big skate may move over an acre or two of seabed and at a fair depth. In the wilderness of stones and rocks, trailing weeds and slowly waving fronds, he has to find your small mackerel. He tastes the water. He has what the shark has, an ability to scent blood and to track down his food. He moves along like a hunting dog. On his way he may come across more distracting scents and more obvious prey so that you need to learn to be patient.

When you discover something heavy on the end of your line you will be almost convinced that your trace has become entangled in a wreck. If the big one moves he may only move a few feet to get a better hold. Now you will have to make up your mind to put all the strain on the line it will bear. Many a skate fisherman trying his hand for the first time has moved his fish and thought he had hooked a piano!

The thornback doesn't present such a problem, although since he is more often taken from the shore his sliding away on the running tide can be the undoing of the angler. Once he settles he has to be dislodged. The farther out he manages to get, the less chance the angler has. Drag him up and he may turn over and the hook will be ripped out.

A final problem awaits the angler who brings his thornback home. It has to be skinned. The thorns are real and there are whorls of cartilage in the body of the fish. The skin is not only as prickly as a cactus, but rough. It is first eased off with a knife and then it may be torn away.

Having discarded the skin and the inedible parts, think yourself lucky to have a fish that cooks so well in golden batter. It is a fish fit for a king although not many kings may have had it set before them! It is, after all, shark meat and this has only been popular among the poor, who have kept the secret of its tastiness to themselves.

FISHING FACTS

Tickets, Licences and Seasons

There are so many variations from one part of the country to the next, so far as tickets and licences are concerned, that it would be impractical to attempt to list them all. In some places salmon fishing begins in January and in others not until after March. In England and Wales licences are required for brown trout as well as for sea trout and salmon, but in Scotland no licence is needed for brown trout. Coarse fish may be taken in some River Board areas and in others coarse fishing is as strictly controlled as game fishing and leased to clubs or associations of angling clubs. The would-be angler must enquire at the tackle shop or from the owner of any water he may arrange to fish to ensure that he is complying with the law and not poaching. The right to fish can never be assumed because someone says that the water is free. The owner may not require a fee but the River Board may insist upon a licence and prosecute any-one who flouts its byelaws.

Put-and-take fisheries in which trout of a takeable size have been stocked, even though they are private concerns, still come under the River Board for licence purposes. Coarse fishing waters are controlled to protect the species during the 'close' season between March and June. Coarse fish may be taken away and used for the pot but many associations, particularly in the heavily fished waters of the southern counties, insist upon the fish being put back. This is a practice in the interests of sport and one which may one day apply through-out Britain. Here and there the eager angler will nevertheless encounter fishing authorities who will allow him to fish for coarse fish – pike, perch and rudd, because they are predatory or compete with trout – only on condition that the catch is *not* returned to the water. While the experienced coarse fisherman will deplore the ultimate loss of sport such a regulation involves, in these circum-stances the quality of game fishing is the principal object.

How to Identify Your Fish

The newcomer to fishing quickly discovers that fish have many distinguishing features and he is never likely to confuse a pike with a carp or a bream with a tench. He soon learns why a mirror carp is so-called (it has large and rather ugly scales) and he comes to know that the brassy looking fish with red adornment is a rudd, and the roach to which it has a certain resemblance is silvery but lacks the large 'keel' of the rudd.

With all their distinguishing features all fish have the same means of loco-motion. They are fitted with fins which propel them along, enable them to brake and reverse and keep upright in the water. Fins may vary from one species to another because of the way in which a fish lives. A predator like a pike must have a broad tail because it is the tail that gives him his rapid take-off. A perch, feeding in different levels of the lake or pond, and sometimes in the river, balances by means of a large dorsal fin equipped with spines in case he is seized by a greedy fish of larger size. He also has a secondary dorsal fin to make his balancing perfect.

While game fish, salmon, sea trout and browns also have a dorsal fin they have another small fin between the dorsal and the tail which is not a second dorsal but a rayless fin known as the adipose. The real purpose of this fin is hard to understand but fish farmers and researchers often make use of this small fin in marking or tagging fish to discover where they go or how long they remain in the sea when they have migrated.

Beginning at the head of the fish just behind the gill covers we find fins known as the pectorals. Almost immediately below this pair of fins are the ventrals. Both sets of fins are rudder-shaped and eminently designed for steering. The dorsal lies along the back of the fish and is complementary to the anal fin on the underside of the body in front of the tail. The tail fin is known as the caudal. Fish may swim up through the water or down into it, but to enable them to maintain their position they need to inflate and deflate what is known as a swim bladder which compensates for the difference in pressure encountered in moving from the surface to the deeps or vice versa. The fish occasionally hauled up from very deep water suffers similar distress to a diver surfacing too quickly despite this built-in decompression device. A fish breathes through the membrane of its gills, extracting oxygen from the water in a way similar to the operation of human lungs which extract oxygen from air we breathe in.

Where to Find Your Fish

Sea fish in general: Almost every clean beach and inshore area around Britain can provide fish. Some areas in the south and south-west are particularly noted for bass and tope. Shark fishing is done off Cornwall and Southern Ireland.

Coarse fish in general: Coarse fish are widely distributed throughout Britain although a greater variety of species is available to the angler in southern Britain.

Game fish in general: Clean rivers of both the eastern and western parts of northern England, the rivers of Wales and south-west England and all the rivers of Scotland and Ireland, as well sea lochs and inland lochs with rivers providing access to the sea, have salmon or sea trout and often both species. Many lakes and streams in the same areas have good trout fishing and in some reservoirs trout fishing is exceptionally good.

Baits to Catch Your Fish

Sea fish in general: General purpose baits are ragworm, lugworm, soft crab, prawn, squid, mussel and limpet. Lures and feathers called mackerel flies are effective for pollock as well as mackerel. Spoons and other revolving metal devices take most predatory fish both in salt and fresh water.

Coarse fish in general: Maggot, breadcrust, potato, worm, paste, and cheese are most often used for coarse fishing in combination with cloud and ground bait. Predatory coarse fish are taken on live and dead bait (minnows etc). and on spoons and spinners of every sort, and on flies.

Game fish in general: Game fish are fished for with fly, spinners, dead minnows, worms, prawn and shrimp.

Suggestions for Further Reading

Bartles, Bill, *Match Angling* (A. & C. Black Ltd, 1972).

Clarke, Brian, *The Pursuit of Stillwater Trout*, (A. & C. Black, 1975).

Falkus, Hugh, *Sea Trout Fishing* (H. F. & G. Witherby Ltd, 1962).

Hilton, Jack, *Quest for Carp* (Pelham Books Ltd, 1972).

Kite, Oliver, *Nymph Fishing in Practice* (Barrie & Jenkins Ltd, 1963).

Mohan, Peter, *Carp For Everyone* (David & Charles, 1972).

Scott, Jock, *Salmon and Trout Fishing up to Date* (Seeley, Service & Co. Ltd, 1960).

Smith, Cyril. *Coarse Fishing Today* (G. Bell & Sons Ltd, 1957).

Stoker, Hugh, *The Modern Sea Angler* (Robert Hale & Co., 1971).

Venables, Bernard, *Freshwater Fishing* (Barrie & Jenkins, 1967).

Wrangles, Alan, *Complete Guide to Sea Angling* (Newnes, 1967).